Saudi Real Estate Law
and
Practice

Saudi Real Estate Law and Practice

by
Michael O'Kane

2013

Publisher's Cataloging-In-Publication Data
(Prepared by The Donohue Group, Inc.)

O'Kane, Michael, 1955–
    Saudi real estate law and practice / by Michael O'Kane.

    p. ; cm.

    Includes index.
    ISBN: 978-0-9910476-1-1

    1. Real property– –Saudi Arabia– –Handbooks, manuals, etc.
2. Mortgages– –Saudi Arabia– –Handbooks, manuals, etc.   3.
Real property– –Finance– –Law and legislation– –Saudi Arabia–
–Handbooks, manuals, etc. I. Title.

KMT683 .O53 2013
346.538043

CONTENTS

ACKNOWLEDGMENTS

The author would like to thank Dr. David Ball, formerly of Riyadh and Jeddah and more recently, Oman, for permitting the liberal use of his unpublished 2007 paper reviewing certain Saudi real estate laws. I would also like to thank Christopher Johnson of the Law Firm of Mohamed Al-Sharif in Riyadh for valuable input into Saudi real estate procedures. Any errors in the text, however, are solely my own

INTRODUCTION

It has been a little more than a year since Saudi Arabia enacted a series of laws to stimulate and strengthen the country's real estate sector. The laws have been slow in coming. The first draft of the Registered Mortgage Law was published in the Saudi Gazette newspaper in 2008. The general consensus among economists, banks, foreign investors and government officials was that the news laws would lead to greater lending, construction and trade in the real estate sector. Saudi Arabia has a growing population and its future housing needs must be met.

None of these projections have come true—yet. No one seems to know why. The October, 2013 crackdown on foreign labor will certainly have an impact on construction. But at the time of this writing the planned system is barely operating, if at all. Part of the reason is due to both the size and the novelty of the system. Most commentators introduce the fact of the new laws by asserting that there are but five new laws. This is grossly inadequate. There are five Saudi regulations termed "laws" but each of these has an Implementing Regulation with the force of law. One of these, the Implementing Regulations for the Execution Law, have not yet been issued. It is important to keep in mind that all Saudi "laws" are but regulations, subordinate to the Holy Qu'ran and the traditions of the Prophet. Even the country's constitution, or Basic Law, is a regulation in this sense.

The nine new regulations contemplate the creation of entities which have not yet been created and the further promulgation of rules governing the conduct of these entities. While such rules are in development and progress has been made, what I would like to call the new Saudi mortgage ecosystem—for it is indeed a system and not merely five new laws—has yet to be inaugurated.

When the new system is fully functional, new procedures will govern the purchase and sale of real estate in the country. Previously, real estate transfers were a private matter. The state had a limited role. Records were not public. Collection of debt in a system where the lack of interest removed any incentive to pay on time has always been problematic. Now the courts have been empowered to aggressively redeem unpaid debts. Whether the courts will use these powers is another matter.

In the past, the Saudi judiciary has sometimes been reluctant to implement business-friendly laws. Because of this reluctance, the government was forced to detour around the courts and form quasi-judicial committees to enforce contracts. Indeed, the Supreme Judicial Council in 1981 prohibited notaries and judges from registering any mortgage issued by a commercial bank. The order was entered because a hadith of the Prophet condemned the "writer" of a usurious loan. The Council made a factual finding that mortgages granted by commercial banks violate the Islamic shari'a. *See* Vogel, *Islamic Law and Legal System*, (New York: Brill Academic Publishers, 2000). The result was diminished use of commercial bank mortgages and the creation of a disputes committee within the country's Central Bank, SAMA, to enforce commercial loans.

Thirty years later, SAMA has been tasked to try again. This time the law provides that commercial mortgages must be compliant with the Islamic shari'a. Nevertheless, in all instances except one, disputes arising from commercial mortgages will be resolved by a new SAMA committee instead of the courts. The SAMA committee has powerful remedies at its disposal, such as blacklisting a person from the banking system, but ultimately these remedies are limited.

Perhaps the most important real estate law in Saudi Arabia is not directly concerned with property. The new Execution Law was enacted at the same time as the other new mortgage laws and is an important component of the Saudi property ecosystem. The simple purpose of this law is to ensure that there will be consequences when borrowers do not pay their debts.

The sole instance where the judiciary will still play a role in the new mortgage system is with respect to enforcement. While no new court has been created, the government created a new division within the courts that amounts to the same thing. This new court is called an Execution Court. The Execution Court's remit extends to the enforcement of all judgments and not just those involving mortgages. The Execution Court judge has access to those remedies traditionally wielded by the judiciary, including the power to imprison.

The Execution Law is thus an extremely important component of the new system. Because its jurisdiction extends to all judgments and not simply foreclosures and evictions, it is not likely that the Supreme Judicial Council will repeat their prohibitions as it did in 1981.

Islamic finance is particularly suited to the real estate industry. The reason for this is that in the real estate business there is always a physical property which is bought or sold. Even collateralized debt obligations were based, ultimately, on the existence of physical property. While it is not widely recognized, all Islamic finance transactions involve the existence of a property or collateral. That is, any Islamic finance transaction cannot be deemed to be compliant with the Islamic shari'a without the existence of a property of some kind. Since real estate transactions always involve physical property, the use of shari'a compliant Islamic financing vehicles should be widespread. For whatever reason, this is not yet the case. Instead, Western mortgage and interest based models are often seen as the foundation for an unnatural Islamic finance structure. This need not be the case. Saudi Arabia anticipates that its new real property industry will be shari'a compliant and there is no reason why it cannot be.

When the new mortgage system is fully operational its goals are likely to be met. Of this there is little doubt. The issue is whether the system will become operational, and one year after enactment of nine laws and counting, that remains to be seen.

CHAPTER 1

SAUDI ARABIA'S NEW MORTGAGE ECOSYSTEM

1.1 Introduction

In medieval England real estate buyer and seller together walked the boundaries of land to be conveyed. If the terms were satisfactory, the seller picked up a clod of earth and handed it to the buyer. Such was the system by which real property was transferred.

At the time of the Prophet Mohammad, Arabia was a traditional society in which custom and oral evidence were sufficient to support a claim to property.

The Ottoman Land Code of 1858 followed by the Land Registration Law of 1859 became law in what was then known as the Kingdom of Hijaz in what is now Western Saudi Arabia. Requirements concerning registration and the use of title deeds were mostly ignored. There was no cadastral survey and it was often impossible to determine a property's boundaries. In the rest of Saudi Arabia, at best only nominally under Ottoman control, traditional customs and practices were preferred.

Today real property transfers are complex mechanisms which serve various social and political interests. Buyer and seller no longer stand alone in a field. The State has an interest in taxation and discouraging nuisances as well as the soundness of its currency. Those who govern the State must promote the availability of housing for the governed. Real estate may be a business, a passive investment or a consumable. These competing and complementary interests are seen in one or another aspect of conveyancing. Conveyancing itself is a snapshot of the system as a whole.

For the past several years the Saudi business and financial communities have urged passage of a new mortgage regime to facilitate financing of land transfers and as a business opportunity. Interest in the Kingdom's vast lands is intense. Despite the Kingdom's size and low population density, housing shortages are endemic. In many ways, Saudi Arabia's land system appears feudal and vast tracts of undeveloped land are found even in the cities. Property transfers are privately concluded before notaries and there is no easy way to determine ownership of a tract of land.

The lure of profit and need for new housing were motivation enough for change. In July, 2012 the Kingdom announced that a new mortgage law had been approved. Details were not immediately forthcoming. Religious conservatives wondered how there could be conventional mortgages in a legal system which prohibits interest. Months passed and now it has become clear why those details were not immediately released, for what was passed was not a single law but an entire credit and financing ecosystem.

Implementing a system of mortgages in the Kingdom required the establishment of an entire infrastructure, an infrastructure that previously had been lacking. The new mortgage ecosystem not only provides for financing real property but establishes institutions and entities which are needed for the system to operate efficiently.

1.2   Features

The law approves real estate mortgages as long as they comply with the Islamic shari'a. The law does not attempt to stifle financial innovation by prescribing one type of Islamic mortgage over another, but contains consumer protection and other provisions which all compliant mortgages will be required to contain.

The Saudi Arabian Monetary Agency ('SAMA') will be the overseer of the new ecosystem. SAMA will license and regulate the new entities created by the law as well as the forms of transaction and the types of financial products. A framework for non-bank financing companies is provided for.

The proposed Saudi mortgage system provides for the public dissemination of price and sales data and the use of such information to assist in the valuation of similar properties to discourage fraud while promoting the soundness of the system. The system provides for the registration of deeds in public registries. Registration, coupled with title insurance, will help resolve those thorny questions of ownership which have made collateralization and verification difficult in the Kingdom. For the first time, credit and title insurance are recognized and approved as essential components of real estate conveyancing.

The Real Estate Development fund will help provide liquidity to the system. The possibility of tax incentives is provided for as well as the possibility of new financial products, subject to SAMA approval. Mortgages and other debt obligations may be securitized. A new court will be established to hear and adjudicate real estate financing disputes.

1.3 Credit Bureaus and Reports

The first new entity populating the new ecosystem is the credit bureau. There are already private credit bureaus in existence in Saudi Arabia as well as a banking and credit blacklist maintained by SAMA itself. Credit reports will play an important role in real estate financing in Saudi Arabia. The creditworthiness of Saudi citizens and companies will now be open to scrutiny. This is a major sea change. In the past these matters were kept private. Now, every real estate conveyancing must be documented with the Borrower's credit report. In Saudi Arabia, the reputational or character loan has long been a principal feature of financing. This will no longer be the case.

1.4   Real Estate Finance Companies

Real estate finance companies will be established as joint stock companies with a minimum capital requirement of SAR 500 million. The maximum amount of credit facilities granted for each company is five times the company's capital. These companies will be strictly regulated by SAMA, with SAMA requiring and approving the company's five year business plans, financial products, composition of the board and key officers. According to SAMA rules, each financing company must have an outside auditor and separate internal audit, credit, risk and compliance committees. To facilitate dealing with the public, the finance company must also have a complaints department.

There are restrictions on loans to a single borrower (20%) in the absence of a waiver from SAMA. Upon formation, real estate finance companies must have at least 50% Saudi national employees. This should not be difficult given that the Saudi banking sector is–and has been–Saudiized at a rate of 90% or more for years, but it means that competition for qualified candidates will be keen. There must be a 5% increase in the percentage of Saudis hired until fully 75% of the new company's employees are Saudi nationals.

Except where loans are in the amount of SAR 100,000 or less, loans must be 100% collateralized. Only 10% of a company's loans may be no collateral loans. On-spec real estate loans need SAMA approval in advance.

Assuming that the company makes a profit, it must seek SAMA approval before a dividend can be paid.

1.5   Saudi Real Estate Refinancing Company

This new entity is a hybrid public/private entity formed by the Saudi Public Investment Fund which will be the 51% owner. The purpose of the company is to provide liquidity secondary markets. It will have a capital of 2 billion SAR and will be listed on the Saudi stock market within five years, if approved by SAMA. It cannot directly finance Borrowers but can finance real estate finance companies. The company may hold and manage investments as well as issue bonds or sukuk. The company can purchase securitized mortgages which can be sold as private placements under CMA rules to qualified individuals and institutions.

1.6 Title and Credit Insurance

The licensing of cooperative insurance companies is already provided for under Saudi law. What is not known is whether companies that are already licensed will seek SAMA approval to offer these new products or form subsidiaries or new companies to offer them. It is also not known to what extent SAMA will permit these companies to obtain reinsurance on world markets. Since the purchase of reinsurance has previously been seen in Saudi commercial transactions, it is likely that the same will apply here.

1.7 Recording Office

In most countries the Registrar of Deeds or title recording office is a government office. This will not be the case in Saudi Arabia. While regulated by SAMA, a private company will be formed by the yet to be licensed Finance Companies as shareholders. Regulations to be issued will govern to what extent information held by the recording offices are accessible by members of the public or other lenders. At least initially, consent by a borrower to the sharing of this information with credit bureaus should be a condition of any loan facility. If a mortgage is securitized that fact should be recorded. This appears to solve the problem of not having a central registry for securitized mortgage notes, a problem that has plagued some Western countries.

1.8   Recovery Companies

Recovery companies are specialized companies that will be licensed by the Ministry of Justice. No such companies currently exist. What is not clear is whether collection companies will arise to collect debts as well and whether these will need Ministry of Justice licensing.

1.9   Loan Service Companies

These companies must be licensed by SAMA as well. The loan servicing function may be performed by a Finance company, but if a company is going to service loans without making them it will need separate SAMA licensing.

1.10   Dispute Resolution

Of all the new entities, probably the easiest for SAMA to establish and work with is the specialized court for Real Estate disputes. SAMA already has a good deal of experience with such tribunals, managing both the Negotiable Instruments Committee and the Banking Disputes Committee. Both of these administrative tribunals have won good reputations in the Kingdom as fair, efficient tribunals where debts can be settled. Unlike other courts in the Kingdom, these two existing tribunals are known to enforce contracts as written, even in the contracts provide for the payment of interest. One can expect the same treatment with respect to real estate mortgage contracts which, while eschewing the word 'interest', include what is called a 'term cost'. What is not clear is whether this new court will have jurisdiction over property seizures and evictions.

1.11 Conclusion

The establishment of a real estate financing ecosystem is designed to facilitate badly-needed growth in the housing sector while seeking to stabilize prices across the country. Lenders will no longer fear that loans on real estate are essentially uncollateralized and unprotected and that borrowers can avoid their debts without fear of execution.

Eventually there will be uniformity across the Kingdom as best practices propagate downwards from SAMA, the regulator. Once there is an approved way of doing things, that way will be adopted throughout the country. There will be transparency in loan documentation since SAMA will approve the forms. Due diligence will become routine since real estate prices will be published and credit bureau reports standardized.

Securing collateral for debt obligations will become standardized and transparent in the Kingdom. The validity of financial instruments will no longer be left to judgments of individual religious scholars but the collective will of the nation. While at first the effects will be seen most easily in the real estate sector, in time there will be other effects. Businessmen will find it easier to obtain financing by factoring receivables. To the extent the economy has been held back due to the prohibition on interest its substitution with other financial instruments and recognition will increase the velocity of money. Previously unavailable financing sources will now be available, opening the economy to new business.

There will be negative consequences as well. The new law calls for the formation of monopoly-like structures which are outside the direct control of the State. In time, this lack of control may prove inconvenient. There will be winners as well as losers. Businessmen will probe the chain of rules in search of weak links. Where weakness is found mischief, and perhaps fortunes will be made.

Greater transparency means loss of privacy in a society which views the private home as a place of almost Embassy-like inviolability. Records will be kept on individuals to an extent and degree heretofore unimagined in the Kingdom and failure to participate will mean being cut off from the credit markets.

And finally, in a way previously unimagined, average citizens will find themselves participating in an unfamiliar new system that is not forgiving of error. Financial maturity will be required. A home which collateralizes an unrelated debt can now be seized–and efficiently so–if a debt is not paid. The spectacle of Saudis losing the family home because of unsuccessful unrelated financial wagers will become commonplace.

The rules of the game have clearly changed and only time will tell whether Saudi society can tolerate all the changes the new system will bring.

CHAPTER 2

REAL ESTATE TRANSFERS IN SAUDI ARABIA

2.1 General

The concepts of freehold and leasehold ownership are not strictly defined in Saudi law. Nevertheless, the basic concepts and attributes of ownership are respected. Leasehold interests are not subject to any registration requirement. Freehold interests must be registered with an individual Saudi notary public who is responsible for land transfers locally.

There are no regulations specifically governing either residential or commercial leases in Saudi Arabia. A lease is treated as any other contract and is subject to the general principles of the Islamic shari'a. The landlord is subject to a basic obligation to allow the tenant quiet possession of the premises, while the basic obligation of the tenant is to pay the rent and preserve the premises in good condition. A lease of property that is not yet in existence will be void. A lease or purchase of an option to lease is permitted. There is no automatic renewal right at the end of the leasehold, though these can be included in the contract. While it was not always the case, currently residential property is commonly rented only on an annual basis with the full amount of the lease paid in advance. Landlords thus have little incentive to provide services to tenants as tenants cannot withhold rent in case of non-performance. There is a shortage of properties available for rental. Unimproved land appreciates in value so there is little incentive to sell or develop.

There are no specific taxes levied on real estate transactions. There is, however, an older and disregarded law which provides for the imposition of a tax on the transfer of real property. This law has fallen into disuse but has not been abolished.

Traditionally, the acquisition of land and buildings involved a privately negotiated transaction between the two parties, often involving a real estate agent. Deeds were handwritten an not registered. A contract is prepared on behalf of the seller who provides that document to the prospective buyer usually with information regarding in the land. The contract contains the commercial terms of the transaction. Negotiated provisions concern the level of disclosure by the seller and the seller's representations and warranties supporting that disclosure. In the absence of a valid objection, title deeds proved ownership. Because of the private nature of the transaction, the likelihood of any objection or even the dissemination of the fact of the sale is remote.

Except for general shari'a contract rules, the seller is generally not obliged to disclose any particular information concerning the land or building to the buyer. The failure to disclose information concerning the state of the property, details of ownership and tenant leases usually causes a request for further information. Here the seller must be careful since the existence of undisclosed, hidden defects may vitiate the contract under general shari'a contract principles as caveat emptor has no place in the Islamic law of contract.

As a practical matter it is very difficult to carry out due diligence in the Kingdom. Until the land registry is established, it is difficult or impossible to conduct a successful search of local government agencies and records for real estate information. Further, the actual ownership of land, and whether there are any dealings affecting that land, can really only be confirmed at the stage when the notary public becomes involved in the registration process.

This has led to the practice of sham contracts where the buyer involves the notary public with a simulated sale in order to access the notary's records. To say that this is inefficient is an understatement but the practice well describes the current reality of real estate transfers in Saudi Arabia in those areas where the registry has not been established.

2.2 Traditional Procedures To Transfer Real Estate

- The legal representatives of the buyer and seller appear before the local notary public in the area where the realty is located. The representatives of both parties must provide copies of any relevant articles of association (or personal identity papers) to confirm capacity and the seller provides the original title deed.
- The notary public sends the original title deed to the records department clerk to ensure authenticity of the title deed. The notary public records that transaction on the record of transfer.
- The parties then sign the record before the notary public.
- The local registrar copies details of the transaction in the title register held by the local notary public.
- The notary public issues a new title deed (or in some cases endorses the existing deed) in the name of buyer (including the transaction details) to the buyer or his legal representative.

The notary public plays a key role in all land transfers in Saudi Arabia. The Executive Regulations of Notaries Public Jurisdictions, issued by Ministry of Justice Circular No 13/T/2460 dated 25/5/1425H (13/7/2004) grant the notary public the express power to certify estate ownership transfers as well as mortgages affecting real estate.

2.3 Current Procedures To Transfer Real Estate

Role of Notary Public Department

In Riyadh, transfers take place at the Notary Public Department ("NPD"). Established in 2007, the NPD operates and manages a full service electronic system for the registration of transfers of ownership.

Procedural Steps–Role of Notary Public/Notary Public Department–First Meeting

(a) Seller and Buyer (or their legal representatives) go to the NPD together.

(b) The NPD provides Seller and Buyer with a transfer note which identifies the property and its recorded value.

(c) Seller and Buyer then take the transfer note to a meeting with an available notary public.

(d) Seller and Buyer present to the notary public:
   (i) (if their party is a company), a copy of the Articles of Association;
   (ii) (if their party is an individual), personal identity papers; and
   (iii) documents evidencing the authority of each representative to appear before the notary public on behalf of the buyer and seller respectively (if applicable).

(e) The Seller produces the original title deed in his name.

   Under the ministerial circular, the notary public must rely on the original copy of the deed, and nothing else (Article 13).

(f) The notary public then reviews and verifies:
   (i) the articles of association of the parties, to ensure the capacity of the parties to buy and sell the particular property;
   (ii) the original title deed, to ensure ownership by the seller;
   (iii) the parties' representatives powers of attorney; and
   (iv) the initial transfer note showing the recorded value of the property.

(g) Once satisfied that all documents are in order, the notary public will electronically transfer the transaction information to the Records Department

Further Procedural Steps–Role of Records Department

The Records Department then:

(a) enters transaction details into the title register;
(b) prepares a new title deed containing transaction details showing the buyer as the owner of the property
(c) electronically enters the new title in the Record Department's register of all title deeds in Riyadh.

Second Meeting before Notary Public

Seller and Buyer (or their representatives) then return to the notary public who:

(a) prints a copy of the new title deed showing the buyer as owner;
(b) requires the Seller and Buyer, or their legal representatives, to sign a standard form sale agreement in the presence of two male Muslim witnesses;
(c) gives the new title deed to the buyer or his representative;
(d) scans the sale agreement into the records files; and
(e) retains the original sale agreement.

The buyer then must appear personally before the notary public to sign a confirmation of receipt of the title deed.

CHAPTER 3

ADDITIONAL REAL ESTATE LAWS

3.1 Law of Ownership and Partitioning of Real Estate Units

Ministerial Resolution No. 40 dated 9/2/1423H (22/4/2002)

Condominium ownership of real property is permitted under The Law of Ownership and Partitioning of Real Estate Units, Ministerial Resolution No. 40 dated 9/2/1423H. The law also provides for the partitioning of existing property. The costs of maintenance must be shared amongst the owners.

If a condominium has more than ten units and five owners a condominium association must be formed and registered. Such an association has its own legal personality. Interestingly enough, though Saudi Arabia is an absolute monarchy, condominium associations are perhaps the only national entities governed by their limited electorate. Because Islam has long permitted women to hold their own property, women were first permitted to vote in matters of condominium association affairs even though they could not vote in the elections for the advisory national assembly.

Article 7 of the law provides that condominium property can be bought and sold using notarized deeds. At the time, this was somewhat of an innovation. The gradual roll-out of a national property registry has extended this innovation to the rest of the country. Unfortunately, national implementation has not yet been achieved.

3.2   Law of Government Rentals and Eviction from Real Estate

Council of Ministers Resolution No. 234 dated 16/9/1427H (9/10/2006)

The Law of Government Rentals and Eviction from Real Estate was enacted pursuant to Council of Ministers Resolution No. 234 dated 16/9/1427H (9/10/2006) and governs property leased by the government. The regulation forbids the government from renting real estate except in cases of extreme necessity. Unfortunately, the law does not provide much guidance as to what circumstances might constitute "extreme necessity." The government may rent housing for its employees at market rates where the employees' labor contracts entitle them to housing. The landlord must own his property pursuant to a shari'a deed. Presumably registration of a deed under the national registration system will suffice.

The law defines "major leases" as those where the rental amount is more than SAR 200,000 per annum. For these leases, the amount of rent that can be charged the government is subject to a maximum based on the appraised value of the property. For most types of property, the rent may not exceed 10% of the appraised value. For hospitals, security checkpoints and schools the rent may not exceed 12% of the appraised value.

Leases may not exceed three years but may automatically renew unless the counterparty gives 180 days notice of his intention not to renew. In the event of renewal, the rent paid by the government can be increased by a maximum of 5% for one year renewals or 10% for renewals longer than one year. The total term of a lease, including renewals, may not exceed twelve years.

At the end of the lease, the government is responsible for repairing air conditioning as well as restoring electrical and water utilities if the connections have deteriorated during the lease term. The law provides for an end of lease meeting between the government's representative and the lessor. If the landlord fails to appear for the end of lease meeting, the government may return the keys to the municipality and will have no further liability to the landlord. Otherwise, the government tenant remains liable for the misuse of the property. The amount of compensation is decided by an administrative disputes resolution committee rather than the courts.

3.3 Real Estate Appropriation by Citizens of GCC States

(issued in implementation of the Declaration of the 20th Session of the Supreme Council of GCC States, dated 29 November 1999)

GCC citizens may own property in Saudi Arabia, subject to various restrictions. According to Articles 1 and 2 of this law, any citizen of the GCC may own up to 3000 square meters of property for a personal residence but for no other purpose. If the GCC citizen is naturalized, he must be naturalized for at least ten years before being permitted to acquire land in Saudi Arabia. If the land purchased is unimproved, construction must begin within three years and finish within five. The GCC national property owner must hold the property for at least eight years before he is permitted to sell. There are no restrictions on GCC nationals leasing property. This is not a special right since aliens who possess a Saudi residence permit or iqama may also lease property without restriction.

3.4 Ownership and Investment in Real Estate by Non-Saudis

Royal Decree No. M/15 dated 17/4/1421H (20/7/2000)

Foreign interest in obtaining or mortgaging Saudi property has increased the significance of the Regulation of Ownership and Investment in Real Estate by Non-Saudis, Royal Decree No. M/15 dated 17/4/1421H (20/7/2000). This law was enacted around the time of the push by Saudi Arabia to join the World Trade Organization and the passing of the Foreign Investment Law. This law is an adjunct to the Foreign Investment Law but the law has taken on greater importance due to the passage of the package of at least nine laws creating a new Saudi mortgage ecosystem. Foreign real estate developers, sensing a new market, are eager to jump in. Whether they can do so or not depends on the terms of this law.

In keeping with its purpose, the law provides that a foreign investor who has been licensed by SAGIA, the Saudi Arabian General Investment Authority may own property in his own name to conduct his business and house his employees and himself. If the foreign investor is engaged in building construction, the value of the land must be at least SAR 30 million. Those foreigners who have a residency permit in the Kingdom (called an iqama) can purchase land as well, provided that a license is obtained from the Ministry of the Interior. In all other cases, the Minister of the Interior may grant permission to foreigners to own real estate in the Kingdom.

Saudi practice has been not to grant permission to own property to foreigners. Even after passage of this law, that permission was granted in only isolated cases. In fact, an informal poll of major law firms in the Kingdom taken in August, 2012 failed to identify a single client who had been successful in purchasing real estate after having been given a license by SAGIA to do so. The Kingdom does from time to time offer political asylum to individuals but these are not commercial cases.

It is important to remember in this context that Saudi nationality is based on the principle of *jus sanguinis* flowing through the father. Being born in Saudi Arabia is insufficient to confer Saudi nationality as is having only a Saudi mother. There are expatriate families, among them Palestinian, who have lived in the Kingdom for several generations without obtaining Saudi nationality. Curiously, in the early 1960s, before the oil shock of 1974, Saudi citizenship was offered for sale.

The law confirms the well-known principle that real estate in Mecca and Medina may not be owned by non-Saudis except where the property is acquired through inheritance. Property so inherited by a non-Saudi is not taken in fee but as a life estate. Similarly, there are restrictions on the leases of real property in the holy cities. Non-Saudis may only lease land for a period not to exceed two years.

3.5 Realty in Kind Registration Law

Royal Decree no. 6 dated 11/2/1423H(24/4/2002)

The Realty in Kind Registration Law (the meaning is "real property registration law") provides for the establishment of a nationwide system of centralized registration of title to plots of land. Articles 6 to 8 set out the basic structure of the registry. The primary basis for registration is the so-called "realty unit" – perhaps more accurately translated as "subdivision," which is further divided into individual plots or estates, apparently identified by serial numbers (Article 27).

The registration of title is done by allocating a sheet, or folio, to each "realty unit" and inscribing the names of the owners of each of the plots in the realty unit, as well as the charges on that particular plot. In addition, attached to each "realty unit" folio, there is an alphabetical index of all the names of the landowners in that particular subdivision together with the numbers of the plots they own.

According to Article 9, the Ministry of Municipal and Rural Affairs is responsible for identifying the "realty units," setting up the cadastral system, and preparing the maps of each "realty unit," while the Ministry of Justice has the authority to document the rights attributable to each plot of land.

Article 10 is particularly confusing because it seems to provide that the original documents on the basis of which the entries in the registry are made (i.e., title deeds) will be safeguarded in the registry and only competent government officials will have access to review them. Persons doing a title check on a particular parcel of land, therefore, will presumably be unable to look behind the register itself to determine whether the register is accurate. However, it nowhere says that the register is a publicly accessible place.

Article 10 also provides that the underlying documents for lands being used for military installations and "national economic projects" will not be kept in the registry, but in the appropriate governmental department, and will be subject to confidentiality.

Article 15 provides that the provisions of this law are to be applied "gradually," with the first entry being made at such time as the Minister of Justice, after consultation with the Minister of Municipal and Rural Affairs, identifies the realty area in which registration will begin.

According to Article 16, a magistrate will supervise the process of registration after giving 60 days' notice in Umm al-Qura of the commencement of registration for a particular area.

According to Article 23, the Minister of Justice, on recommendation from the magistrate supervising the first entry, can postpone, for up to three years, the demarcation and registration of a particular area when doing so is in the public interest.

Interested parties may object within 60 days following the completion of demarcation or registration (Article 25). This must be read together with Article 29 - which gives interested parties one year to file an objection to the statements or notations made on the registration folio of a particular "realty unit" - and Article 34, which gives parties two years after inscription where new evidence has surfaced that gives grounds for changing what has been inscribed.

All rights related to a parcel of real estate, such as mortgage and pledge, must be inscribed on the appropriate folio (Article 36). Lease agreements must also be recorded (Article 37). Persons who inherit realty cannot dispose of their land until they register it (Article 38). A person claiming a debt against the heir of a particular plot must countersign the register (Article 39).

Articles 60 and 61 provide for the removal of easements, thereby presuming that easements are among the rights that must be recorded against property pursuant to Article 36.

Article 66 provides that each multi-story unit shall be deemed a separate "realty unit" or subdivision. Thus, each apartment building will have a folio to itself, which shows the owner of each apartment, and also presumably has an alphabetical index of the owners' names.

Article 67 provides that each landowner shall be given a copy of the folio on which his ownership is inscribed, and that sheet shall be called a "title deed."

Article 78 provides that this law took effect one year after its promulgation. The process of implementing this law was delayed for a long time and the first area to be surveyed was completed in 2013.

3.6 Law of Expropriation of Real Estate for the Public Interest and Temporary Possession of Real Estate

Council of Ministers Decision no. 31 dated 5/2/1424H (8/4/2003)

The taking of private land for public use, or expropriation, is a familiar principle in most legal systems around the world. Most countries require the payment of just compensation for such a taking. Saudi law stands apart because, as concerns compensation, it distinguishes between expropriated lands within a so-called "development protection zone" and those lying elsewhere. Basically, in development protection zones, the government has the power to expropriate land to construct roads without compensating the owner as long as the owner is left with at least ten thousand square meters (Article 3).

This same article also provides that the government may expropriate land without compensation to construct roads through property that has been subdivided.

3.7   Law of Time-Share Properties

Royal Decree No. M/52 dated 20/8/1427H (14/9/2006)

The Law of Time-Share Properties is a little-known law enacted in 2006 in response to commercial abuses experienced by Saudis both at home and abroad. The law provides that the General Authority for Tourism and Antiquities will regulate all real estate contracts that qualify as time shares. Time-share sellers must be licensed and time-share contracts are regulated. A buyer has ten days within which he can rescind a time-share contract for any reason, assuming full disclosure under the regulations. In the absence of full disclosure, the buyer has three months. One of the interesting provisions of the law is the creation of a time-share property registry, but it appears that the time-share property registry was not in fact created.

Time shares have not been popular in the Kingdom though there is some activity in the two Holy Cities. The law is nevertheless important because time-shares are defined not as merely contracts, but a real property interest. Whenever a time-share is involved, not only the provisions of the new mortgage ecosystem but the protective provisions of this law are likely to apply.

3.8   Lease of Forest and Arable Lands and National Parks

Council of Ministers Resolution No. 1/428 dated 19/2/1421H (24/5/2000)

This law is of interest because historically it was used as a basis to regulate hotels and promote tourism. The law is, by its terms, only applicable to tourism and entertainment development projects. Responsibility for licensing was assigned to the Ministry of Agriculture and Water. Since the passage of the law, this ministry has been restructured and some of its responsibilities privatized. Nevertheless, the investor who seeks to operate hotels in the Kingdom should abide by the licensing regime established under this law until advised otherwise.

3.9 Law of Distribution of Fallow Lands

Royal Decree No. 26, dated 6/7/1388H (29/9/1968)

The Law of Distribution of Fallow Lands was designed to promote agriculture by granting a usufruct to farmers to make unused land productive. As such, it might be considered a specialized or niche piece of legislation were it not for the fact that vacant and unused land is becoming a political issue.

Saudi Arabia is an enormous country and compared to the three main urban centers, is mostly empty. The vacant land, though, is not available for development. One of the reasons for this is that the price of vacant land keeps appreciating at the rate of approximately 15% per year. Thus, there is little incentive for a landowner to sell his property since few investments increase at this rate on a reliable basis. Political pressure is building to either expropriate vacant land from its owners or permit its use in some way. Thus, it is quite possible that this law will assume renewed importance in the future.

3.10   The Law of Roads and Buildings

(published in the Umm al-Qura 1/6/1360H(26/6/1941)

The Law of Roads and Buildings, enacted on 1/6/1360H (26/6/1941) is an older law which might still have applicability in some situations. Saudi laws are not collated or codified. Laws are often enacted for a particular purpose or circumstance, such as the Committee for the Resolution of Debt of Princes and then forgotten. Without a copy of the law and without State Archives or libraries where such laws can be traced, their existence is little more than rumor. Similarly, after a while older laws are seen as archaic simply because of changes of circumstances. Because of these facts it is often difficult to determine what the law of the country is at any given time.

Articles 11-15 of the law deal with government expropriate of real estate and so have been superseded by the Law of Expropriation of Real Estate mentioned in this chapter. The new law, however, did not contain any specific provision to repeal or supersede prior law, and there is nothing in the Saudi Basic Law which provides for automatic repeal or supersession. Other provisions of the law deal with the mapping of cities and thus should be superseded by the Realty in Kind Registration Law, but there is really no way to tell.

Other provisions of the law seem to have been forgotten but could be resurrected at any time. For example, Article 20(a) prohibits the use of any building in a residential area as a shop. Currently, this restriction is ignored. Article 26 requires that all houses must be numbered sequentially. The kindest comment one can make about such a provision is that it is at best aspirational. The law requires technical engineers, architects and contractors to be Saudi nationals but these provisions have been superseded by other laws, including the Contractor Classification Rules and the Professional Engineers Law. Other provisions would seem more appropriate in a construction code. For example, Articles 57-59 deal with the required thickness of walls and Articles 98-99 specify that the minimum floor space required for a dwelling is nine square meters and that windows made in dwellings constructed of mud or a stronger material shall constitute at least 10% of the floor area. Article 77 deals with the separation of structures on jointly owned property. Septic tanks must be constructed at least 20 meters away from water wells.

One look at the magnificent buildings running down Olaya Street in the nation's capital, Riyadh, would cause one to assume that a law addressing buildings made of mud can safely be ignored. In most cases that assumption would be correct, but it is a rule of practicality and not one of law.

3.11   Miscellaneous Real Estate Laws

The Law of the Disposal of Municipal Real Estate

The Law of the Disposal of Municipal Real Estate, Royal Decree No. 64 dated 15/11/1392H (21/12/1972) granted municipalities the power to sell or lease public property to private individuals or entities.

The Real Estate Development Fund Law

The Real Estate Development Fund Law, Royal Decree No. 23 dated 11/6/1394H (2/7/1974) created a government entity to lend money to Saudis to construct their homes or to Saudi companies to build residential complexes. It is expected that the Fund will be a major component of the new Saudi mortgage ecosystem.

The Real Estate Dealers' Offices Regulation

The Real Estate Dealers' Offices Regulation (published in the Okaz newspaper on 26/6/1423H (4/9/2002) requires that all real estate dealers have Saudi nationality. In the past this law was insignificant since the Saudi real estate market was small. As the market grows, it is inevitable that foreign capital will enter the market. The issue will then be whether foreign real estate brokers and salespeople will be allowed to work. It is likely, then, that this law will become increasingly more significant.

Appendices

REAL ESTATE MORTGAGE LAW

(Royal Decree No. m/50 dated 13/8/1433H (3/7/2012)
Preliminary Chapter
Definitions

Article 1

The following words and expressions – wherever stated in this Law – shall have the meanings stated beside them, unless the context requires otherwise:

Law: Real Estate Mortgage Law.

Regulations: Implementing regulations of this Law.

Minister: Minister of Finance.

Agency: Saudi Arabian Monetary Agency.

Ministry: Ministry of Housing.

Real Estate Mortgage Contract: A futures contract related to the ownership of the housing by the beneficiary.

Beneficiary: A natural person obtaining the real estate mortgage service.

Real Estate Financier: Commercial banks and finance companies licensed to engage in real estate mortgage activity.

Consumer: Every person receiving real estate mortgage services.

Person Eligible for Support: Saudi natural person whose income does not exceed the limit proposed by the Minister from time to time, and approved by the Council of Ministers.

Housing Associations: Establishments and charities specialized in providing housing for those who are unable, licensed according to the applicable laws.

Primary Market: Real estate mortgage contracts concluded between the beneficiary and the real estate financier.

Secondary Market: Trading the rights of the financier arising from the primary market contracts.

Chapter I
Supervision and Licensing

Article 2

The Agency shall regulate the real estate mortgage sector, including the following:

1- Allowing banks to engage in real estate mortgage activity by possessing houses to be used in financing–notwithstanding the provisions of paragraph 5 of Article 10 of the Banking Control Law–according to this Law and the regulations.

2- Licensing the real estate mortgage companies according to this Law and the Finance Companies Control Law.

3- Licensing one (or more) joint stock companies for real estate re-mortgage according to the market needs. The Public Investment Fund may contribute to the ownership thereof and the Agency shall approve the candidates for the membership of the Board of Directors and the financiers licensed to contribute in the company's ownership. A part of its shares shall be put for public offering according to the provisions of the Capital Market Law.

4- Licensing the cooperative insurance companies to cover the risks related to real estate mortgage according to the Cooperative Insurance Companies Control Law.

5- Issuing standards and procedures related to real estate mortgage, reviewing the real estate mortgage contracts issued by the real estate financiers, ensuring their conformity to these standards and procedures and achieving the proper protection of the consumer and the beneficiary.

6- Disseminating data related to the real estate mortgage market, handling the development of real estate mortgage techniques, including the techniques of facilitating data flow between the primary market and the secondary market.

7- Determining the principles of disclosing mortgage cost standards and the method of calculation, to enable the consumer to compare prices.

Article 3

The real estate financier shall exercise real estate mortgage activities in a way not violating the provisions of the Islamic Sharia'a, according to the decisions of the Sharia Committees set forth in Article 3 of the Finance Companies Control Law and not violating the integrity of the financial system and justice in dealings.

Article 4

The Ministry of Commerce and Industry, the Ministry of Justice and the Ministry– each in its own competence– shall publish the data related to the real estate market activity, in periodic newsletters, according to the market needs and according to the regulations.

Article 5

The authorities entrusted with the registration of real estate property (Courts and Notaries) shall enable the (licensed) real estate financiers to peruse and obtain the data stated in their real estate registers, as determined by the regulations and in agreement with the Ministry of Justice.

Article 6

The real estate financiers and the real estate mortgage companies shall cover the risks of real estate mortgage by cooperative insurance according to the provisions of the regulations.

Article 7

The beneficiary shall have a credit report at a licensed service provider according to the credit information system, in which the data of his credit history during the mortgage period shall be registered. The regulations and the instructions of the Agency shall determine the minimum limit for the period of the beneficiary's register and the register data during the mortgage period.

Chapter II
Government Support

Article 8

The Real Estate Development Fund shall allocate a part of its approved budget as guarantees and aids for the support of real estate mortgage to the persons eligible for support and the housing associations. The regulations shall organize the method thereof.

Article 9

The Government shall meet the financial obligations entailed on the guarantees of the Real Estate Development Fund to support real estate mortgage, within the extent of the approved guarantees in the Fund's budget.

Article 10

The Council of Ministers may issue a Decision – upon the Minister's suggestion – to grant tax incentives for the investment in the real estate securities.

Chapter III
Secondary Market for the Real Estate Mortgage

Article 11

Without prejudice to the provisions of Article 3 of this Law, the real estate financiers may refinance through the following:

1- Real estate re-mortgage companies according to the provisions of the Law and the regulations.
2- Securities according to the provisions of the Capital Market Law.

Article 12

The mortgage transfer procedures in the real estate mortgage secondary market shall be exempted from the fees of registration in the real estate registration in kind.

Chapter IV
Competencies

Article 13

The competent Court shall settle the disputes arising from the real estate mortgage contracts and shall impose the penalty set forth in paragraph 1 of Article 35 of the Finance Companies Control Law, on whoever proved to be delaying in the settlement of his debt.

Article 14

The Agency shall prepare the regulations of this Law and shall be issued under a Decision by the Minister within ninety days from the date of issuance thereof and it shall enter into effect after the entry into force of the Law.

Article 15

This Law shall enter into effect within ninety days from the date of its publication in the Official Gazette.

THE REGISTERED MORTGAGE REGULATIONS

Chapter 1
Creating the Mortgage

Article 1

1- The registered mortgage: A contract registered according to the terms of these regulations, where the mortgagee (the creditor) acquires an actual right on a specific property that has a register and shall have, according to it, priority on all creditors in recovering his debt from the price of that property, regardless of the party that is holding it.

2- A- If the property registration is done according to the provisions of the Actual Registration of Real Estate Regulations, then the mortgage registration shall take place according to the provisions stipulated in those regulations.

B- The registration of a mortgage applied on a property that does not abide by the provisions stipulated in the Registration of Real Estate Regulations shall take place by initialing its register at the court or before specialized notaries.

3- The effects of the mortgage shall not be applied on third parties, unless by registering it according to what was stipulated in paragraph (2) of this article. The mortgagor shall bare the expenses of the mortgage deed and registration. The expenses – if paid by other that the mortgagor – shall be a part of the mortgage debt and its rank, unless it is decided otherwise.

Article 2

1- The mortgagor shall be the owner of the mortgaged property and be able to dispose of it.

2- The mortgagor may be the debtor himself, or a kind collateral security provider that offers a property for mortgage for the benefit of the debtor, even without his permission.

Article 3

If the mortgagor is not the owner of the mortgaged property, then his mortgage shall depend on a license documented by the owner and the mortgage shall start on the date the license is delivered. If this license is not issued, than the mortgage right shall only be imposed on the property when it becomes owned by the mortgagor.

Article 4

1- The mortgaged property shall be specified and present, or possibly present, in order to make its selling valid.

2- The mortgaged property shall comprise a due diligence mentioned in the mortgage deed itself or a later deal, and be valid for selling independently in a public auction.

3- The property's benefit may be mortgaged independently from the original and the provisions for mortgaging and registering the original shall be taken into account mortgaging.

Article 5

The mortgage shall comprise the outbuildings of the mortgaged property, including buildings, plants and servicing material, as well as new buildings and improvements that came after the mortgage deed, unless it is agreed otherwise, without violating third parties' rights in these outbuildings.

Article 6

The mortgage issued by all the owners of the common property shall remain valid, regardless of whether the mortgaged property is dividable or not.

Article 7

1- If one of the partners mortgages his common share (partly or entirely), then the mortgage shall be applied, after the division, on the sorted part that were left to him.

2- If one of the partners mortgages his common share (partly or entirely), then his share after the division shall comprise parts other than those he mortgaged or those who were partly left to him. The mortgage shall be transferred in parts that are equal in value to those which were originally mortgaged. This part shall be defined and registered following an order by the specialized judge.

3- The sums due to the mortgagor – as a result of equal parts or the price of the mortgaged property – shall be allocated to pay the debt which is guaranteed by the mortgage.

Article 8

The mortgagee participating in the common mortgage may not ask for a division before proving his right of recovery from the mortgaged property, unless with the mortgagor's approval. When the right of recovery from the mortgaged property is proved, the mortgagee shall have the right to ask to sell the mortgaged part in its common form, and to ask for a division, even without the approval of the mortgagor.

Article 9

In exchange of the mortgage, the stated condition is to have a fixed true estate debt, or a promise of a defined debt, or a tangible asset guaranteed by the debtor, or an obligatory debt, such as one that depends on a condition, a future debt or a probable debt, knowing that the value of the guaranteed debt or the maximum value it could finally reach shall be defined in the mortgage deed.

Article 10

Each part of the mortgaged property guarantees the whole debt and each part of the debt is guaranteed by the mortgaged property, unless it is decided otherwise.

Chapter Two
Mortgage Characteristics
The Mortgagor

Article 11

1. If the property is registered according to the Registration of Real Estate Regulations, then the Owner is allowed to dispose of it.
2. If the property is not registered according to the Registration of Real Estate Regulations, then the mortgagor may not dispose of the mortgaged property, unless it is decided otherwise and it is documented in its title deed and register.

Article 12

1. The mortgaged property yields and expenses shall be the owner's responsibility and he shall have the right to manage it as long as it does not violate the mortgagee's right.
2. The yields shall not be mortgaged with the original asset, unless the mortgagee stipulates so.
3. The mortgagor and mortgagee may decide to recover a part of the debt that is subject to controversy from the mortgaged property yields.

Article 13

The mortgagor shall be committed to preserve the safety of the mortgaged property till the date of the debt payment. The mortgagee shall protest to everything that might decrease the value of the mortgaged property, make it subject to destruction or defect. He shall have recourse to regular interim measures that shall guarantee the truth of his right and ask the mortgagor to pay the expenses.

Article 14

1. If the value of the mortgaged property is diminished or if something hinders the mortgagee from taking his right because of destruction, default or maturity, or if this happens because of an infringement, neglect or fraud from the party holding the mortgaged property (whether a mortgagor or a holder), then the mortgagee shall claim a raise of the mortgage with the same amount it was diminished, or offer a mortgaged item similar to the previous one, as long as it is not replaced by a comparable one. Otherwise, the party holding the mortgaged property shall pay the debt according to early repayment standards stipulated in the Finance Companies Regulations.

2. If destruction or diminishing takes place without any encroachment, neglect or fraud from the party having the mortgaged property, then the parts left of the property or its replacements shall remain mortgaged according to their category.

Article 15

1. If the mortgagor is a provider of a collateral security, then execution shall be restricted to the property that is mortgaged from the funds of its owner who is not the debtor.

2. In case of selling the mortgaged property which has a collateral security, then the owner shall refer to the debtor, but shall only do so after implementing measures on the mortgaged property.

Article 16

In case of works that shall expose the mortgaged property to destruction or default, or make it insufficient for guarantee, then the mortgagee shall ask the tribunal to stop these works and take the measures necessary to stop the harm, according to the provisions of the summary jurisdiction.

The Mortgagee

Article 17

In accordance with the provisions related to disposing of debt, the mortgagee may transfer his right to recover the debt and the guaranteeing mortgage to someone else, unless decided otherwise.

Article 18

In case of maturity of the due debt, the debtor shall take his mortgaged property in case of repayment. In case of non repayment, it shall be sold at the demand of the mortgagee. Also, all parties redeeming his debt shall take their share of the price according to their legal and official rank. In case there is a remaining debt imposed on the mortgagee, the partners shall divide what remains of the debtor's money as well as other debtors.

Article 19

A mortgage may not contain the following provisions:

1- To leave the benefits of the mortgaged property to the mortgagee and have the mortgagee recover the yields of the mortgaged property, with the approval of the mortgager, without benefitting from it.

2- To have the mortgagee own the mortgaged property in exchange of his debt, when he does not repay the mortgagor within the prescribed period.

In both cases, the mortgage is invalid.

Article 20

1- If the mortgaged property is registered in accordance with the Actual Registration of Real Estate Regulations, the lease contract issued by the mortgagor to the mortgagee shall not be implemented, unless it is recorded before the registration of the mortgage deed, if the period is not less than five years. Then, the lease contract shall be implemented, even if it is registered after the mortgage deed.

2- If the mortgaged property is not recorded in accordance with the Actual Registration Of Real Estate Regulations, then the mortgagor shall commit to announce – in the mortgage deed – any original or collateral right on the mortgaged property. In case of appearance of rights that affect the mortgagee's right, because of a lack of announcement, then he shall compensate to the mortgagee for any harm. In case the mortgagor has bad faith, then a criminal case shall launched against him according to Anti-Counterfeiting Regulations.

Rights of Third Parties

Article 21
The effect of the registered mortgage in the face of third parties shall apply from the date of registration, unless that third party acquires an actual right on the mortgaged property before registering the mortgage.

Article 22
The mortgage effect shall be restricted to the debt specified in the mortgage document.

Article 23
Any objection on the registered mortgage, in the face of parties that have not have not signed a contract on transferring the guaranteed debt or wavering its rank, should come only after it is recorded in the original mortgage document and the register of the property.

Right of Preference

Article 24

The registered property may be mortgaged to many mortgagees sequentially. The mortgage rank shall be defined through its reference number and date of registration. It shall keep its rank until the information showing its expiry date is registered at the instance specialized in the registration regulations.

The mortgagees' rights shall be recovered from the price of the mortgaged property, or from the money that replaced it according to the rank of each one of them.

Article 25

The mortgagee debtor may waiver his rank by the amount of the debt he owes to another mortgagee debtor in relation with the mortgaged property, in accordance to the provisions decided for the right transfer.

The Right of Tracing

Article 26

The mortgagee has the right of tracing the mortgaged property in the hands of any of its holders, in order to recover his right from them at the date of maturing, in accordance with his rank.

Article 27

A holder of the mortgaged property is any party to whom the ownership of the property was transferred after the mortgage – for any reason – or any other actual right subject to mortgage, without baring a personal responsibility of the debt that is guaranteed by a mortgage.

Article 28

The mortgagee shall take measures of coercive expropriation and selling of the mortgaged property if the debtor does not repay in the due term, after warning the debtor and the holder of the mortgaged property according to the implementation regulations.

Article 29

The holder of the mortgaged property shall repay the mortgage debt and expenses after receiving a warning, knowing that what he paid shall go to the debtor and he shall replace the creditor who has recovered his rightful share of the debt.

Article 30

1- The holder of the mortgaged property has the right of purification of any registered mortgage.
2- The holder shall have this right until the mortgaged property is sold and the sum he paid shall go to the debtor.

Article 31

Coercive expropriation and selling measures shall be applied on the mortgaged property when the debt is not repaid in accordance with the implementation regulations.

Article 32

The holder of the mortgaged property may take part of the procedures aimed at selling it in an auction. If he wins the auction and he pays its price, then he shall be considered as the owner of the property, in accordance with its original title deeds. The mortgaged property shall be purified of any registered right against it, in case the holder pays the price reached at the auction, or in case he deposits the sum in a bank account of the court.

Article 33

If the auction aimed at selling the mortgaged property ends up with the victory of someone other than its' holder, the latter shall acquire its ownership in accordance with the decision stipulating that he won the auction. Thus, he shall receive his right from the holder, regardless of whether the holder entered the auction or not.

Article 34

If the price of the mortgaged property exceeds the value of the registered debt, then the exceeding sums goes to the owner.

Article 35

The holder of the mortgaged property shall object on the debt because of which the property was sold, using the means available for the debtor's objection, in case the debt was registered after the title deed of the holder was.

Article 36

1- The holder shall launch an action for surety on the previous owner within the limits of what the successor refers to concerning the ownership he got from him, in the form of an accumulation or a donation.
2- The holder shall return to the debtor whatever sum he paid exceeding his due, in accordance with a deed stating his right, no matter for what reason the extra sum was paid. He shall replace the creditors whose rights he fulfilled before the debtor, including those to whom the debtor offered insurances, with the exception of the insurances offered by another person.

Chapter Three
Expiration of the Mortgage

Article 37

1. The mortgage follows the debt, so there shall be a mortgage redemption with the expiry of all the debt documented in it.
2. If the debt has expired, then returned for any reason which makes its stay obligatory, then the mortgage shall go back to the way it was with the return of the debt, without affecting the rights acquired by other parties of good faith, within the period that separates the expiry of the debt and its return.

Article 38

1- If the debt, or a part of it, is repaid before its' maturity in accordance between the contractors, or based on the mortgage deed, the law or the judiciary, a part of the debt shall be degraded according to norms of early repayment stipulated in the Finance Companies Regulations.
2- If the debtor fails to repay and the court sells the mortgaged property before the maturity date, it shall order a repayment of the matured settlements to the creditor, and deposit the rest of the sum in a bank account of the court. The debtor shall ask to release the sum in case he pays early what is left of his debt, or presents a bank guarantee to repay the rest of the debt.

Article 39

The registered mortgage shall expire upon foreclosure in accordancewith the regulations, paying its price to the mortgagee creditors according to the rank of each one of them, or depositing the sum in a bank account of the court.

Article 40

The registered mortgage shall expire with the merger in ownership and with the union of the mortgage right and the ownership right in one person's hands, whether it is through the transfer of the mortgaged property's ownership to the mortgagee, or the transfer of the mortgage right to the mortgagor. If there is no more reason for merger in ownership and if its' disappearance has a retroactive effect, then the mortgage shall return to its precious state.

Article 41
The registered mortgage shall expire if the mortgagee has presented a documented waiver, and he may waiver the mortgage right while the debt remains.

Article 42
The registered mortgage shall expire with the destruction of its location, and provisions for the end of the mortgage stipulated in this regulation shall then be applied.

Article 43
The mortgagor and holder shall ask for a mortgage redemption after the expiry of the hearing period of the debt suit documenting the mortgage, stipulated in other regulations.

Article 44
The mortgage shall not end with the death of the mortgagor or the mortgagee, or with loss of eligibility. If one of them dies, then their heirs replace them and if he loses his eligibility, then his guardian shall replace him.

Article 45
The specialized court shall arbitrate in the conflicts arising from the implementation of the provisions of these regulations.

Article 46
This regulation shall come into force after ninety days of the date of their publication in the Official Gazette.

FINANCIAL LEASE LAW

Royal Decree No. M/48 dated 13/8/1433H(3/7/2012)

Preliminary Chapter
Definitions

Article 1

The below mentioned terms – wherever they might occur - shall have the following meanings, unless context dictates otherwise:

The Law: This Financial Lease Law.

Rules: Executive Rules of the Law.

The Agency: Saudi Arabian Monetary Agency.

The Governor: Governor of Saudi Arabian Monetary Agency.

The Contract: Financial Lease Contract.

Lessor: A joint-stock company licensed to conduct financial leasing.

Lessee: The beneficiary of the leased asset under the contract.

Manufacturer: A party that manufactures the leased asset.

Supplier: A party that supplies the leased asset.

Leased Asset: Leasable Movable and immovable properties, utilities, services and intangible assets (e.g. intellectual property).

Essential Maintenance: One that the existence of the asset relies on it customarily.

Operational Maintenance: One that ensures the permanence of the asset's benefits.

Contracts Record: Keeps financial leasing contracts that were concluded or executed in Saudi Arabia. It also keeps sales contracts that result from financial leasing, in addition to all modifications applied to those contracts, according to the provisions of the law.

CHAPTER ONE
Financial Lease Contract

Article 2
A financial leasing contract is a contract in which the lessor leases movable or immovable assets, utilities, services or intangible assets; being its owner, or the owner of its benefits, or being able to gain the possession of it, if the purpose of the lessee is sub-leasing it to a third party by trade, as shown in the executive rules.

While abiding by the laws of real estate possession for non Saudi citizens, it's permissible to transfer the ownership of leased properties according to the contract's terms, either on the condition of suspension of ownership until all contract's payments are made in addition to an optional specified sum, or with a pledge to buy for a nominal amount, or for a sum that was agreed upon in the contract, or for the value of the leased asset at the time of concluding the contract, or as a grant.

Article 3
A hard-copy or an electronic contract must be written between the lessor and the lessee, it shall include data pertaining to them, to the leased asset, its condition, payments and their dates, contract duration and conditions; it is then recorded according to provisions of the law, along with any later modifications.

Article 4
The lessee may define – prior to concluding the contract – the descriptions of the asset in collaboration with the manufacturer, the supplier or the contractor, and the lessee is then liable for the defined

descriptions.

If the descriptions are defined with the lessor's approval, it is, then, non-binding to the lessor except within the limits of his approval.

Article 5

If the lessor authorizes the lessee – in writing – to receive the asset directly from the manufacturer, supplier or contractor, according to the conditions and descriptions mentioned in the contract, the transaction must be conducted in a record that holds the leased asset's condition; according to this, the lessee is responsible for the conditions mentioned in that signed record; and if the manufacturer, supplier or contractor refrains from signing the record, then the lessee has the right of rejecting the asset.

Article 6

The lessee shall meet the payments in the dates that were agreed-upon in the contract, even if he has not benefited from the asset yet, unless that obstruction was caused by the lessor.

It is permissible to set earlier dates for future payments, in case the lessee fails to meet current payments, on the condition of them not exceeding the number of payments he failed to meet in time.

It is permissible to set an early date for a portion of the total sum to be paid, which is paid back to the lessee in case the asset could not be delivered or benefited from for reason unrelated to the lessee.

Article 7

The lessee adheres to using the leased asset for the agreed-upon purposes, and within typical usage limits, and he is held responsible for conducting operational maintenance at his own expense, and according to prevalent technical conduct. While the essential maintenance is conducted at the lessor's expense, unless both parties agree on it being the lessee's responsibility.

The lessee is responsible to inform the lessor (at his address), with occurring issues that affect the utilization of the asset, wholly or partially, as soon as they happen, according to the rules.

Article 8

The lessee is not permitted to apply any changes or modifications to the leased asset, unless he has a written consent from the lessor that contains the nature of the modification, its range and the party having the modification at is expense.

Article 9

The lessee is not held responsible for the depreciation of the asset, unless it is a result of excessive or abusive usage, in which case the lessee affords the value of depreciation with the exception of what is covered by insurance.

The lessor is held responsible for depreciation if it was caused by him, or by compelling circumstances.

The lessor is held responsible for cooperative insurance, as it is not permitted to be an obligation of the lessee.

Article 10

It is permissible to issue securities for lessor's rights, according to rules and conditions set by the Capital Market Authority.

Article 11

The lessee may sub-lease the asset or the right to possession and use of that asset to a third party in accordance with a written consent of the lessor.

Article 12

The lessor is permitted to place a mark on the asset for the purpose of protecting it, including his name, and the contract registry number in the record.

The lessor – his delegate – may inspect the leased asset, to ensure the continuing possession of the lessee of it, while not affecting the lessee's interests, in accordance to the rules and the conditions stated in the contract.

Article 13

If the possession of the asset, or operating it, requires a license, the lessee may head to the relevant authorities with the intent of obtaining that license, in accordance to the contract and the rules of the law.

The lessee affords all fees of obtaining and renewing the license, unless agreed upon otherwise.

Article 14

The lessee is responsible for the damages that results from using the leased asset.

Article 15

Once the lessor sells the leased asset to a third party, the ownership of the contract is transferred along with that of the asset.

Article 16

The lessee may not gain rights that result from the ownership of the leased asset, nor sub-lease it to a third party without a written consent from the lessor.

Article 17

If the leased asset was movable, it remains so, even if it was fixed or appended to real estate.

CHAPTER TWO
Recording

Article 18

1- While abiding by the conventions of firms law, one or more joint-stock companies are established, under license from the agency, with the purpose of registering contracts, and the following tasks:
- Setting up a record for contracts, without breaching the conventions of Real Estate In-kind Registration Law.
- Registering contracts, including data for leased assets, and rights related to it.
- Disclosing the records to certified financing institutions, with a written consent from the lessor.

2- The participation in establishing and owning the contract registering company – mentioned in the previous paragraph - is limited to companies certified to practice financial leasing. And the agency is responsible for how to increase the capital of the contract registering company (by introducing new certified companies as co-owners of this company), and the way the profits are distributed, while abiding by firms law, and the laws and conventions of stock market.

3- The executive rules regulate the procedures of registration, in the contract registering company, in addition to the ownership statement for non-real estate properties, and other data required by the record, and modification/cancellation procedures, the right of others to view the records, the duration of keeping them, the unity of registry data, their exchange and accessing them, and the sum paid for its services.

Article 19

While abiding by real estate ownership laws, registering contracts according to the provisions and the executive rules of the law, asserts the lessor's ownership of the leased asset against others.

In case of registering the contract, the lessor must conduct marking procedures in the record, in accordance to rules and procedures shown in the executive rules.

It is prohibited to argue against others using later modifications of the contract, that has been applied after marking its record.

Article 20

Notwithstanding the provisions of Article 9 of this Law, the lessee shall deliver the leased asset – in the conditions agreed upon in the contract – to the lessor upon termination of the contract, unless the lessee chooses to gain ownership or extend the lease term in accordance to the contract.

Article 21

The lessor may stipulate the right of terminating the contract and regaining the leased asset, if the lessee fails to meet due payments, according to the executive rules, and within what is considered to be just to each of the involved parties.

Article 22

The contract is terminated if the asset is wholly depreciated.

If the depreciation of the asset was partial, and affected benefiting from it, and if the lessor failed to restore the asset to a working state in time, or failed to replace it with a similar asset that the lessee agrees on; the lessee has the right to terminate the contract, or to agree with the lessor on keeping the contract while modifying the rent to compensate for the damages resulting from the asset's partial depreciation; and in case the contract was kept as is, there shall be no fee for the period of repairing the asset, unless the lessee was compensated – through that period – with an asset not less than the original leased one.

If the relevant authorities issued a sentence that prevented benefiting from the leased asset, with the lessor not being the cause of it, the leasing contract is terminated, and the rent is cancelled starting the date of the sentence.

The executive rules determine the standards of what each party is entitled to upon termination (or self-termination) of the contract, in a way that ensures justice for all parties according to legal principles, while considering due insurance compensations.

Article 23
The lessee may – in case the lessor files for bankruptcy, or ceases financial activities – retain the asset in accordance with the contract terms or return the leased asset with the consent of the liquidation agent.

CHAPTER THREE
Violations and Disputes

Article 24
The competent court has jurisdiction to adjudicate dispute arising from the enforcement of the terms and rules of this Law, determining violations and imposing sanctions in accordance with this Law.

Article 25
If the leased immovable assets were not returned in accordance to rules stated in this Law, the lessor may apply to the competent court for an order obliging the lessee to return the leased assets, and the court shall adjudicate such application within thirty days from the date of filing.

According to the provisions of this Law, the lessor may retrieve the movable assets from the lessee in case the contract included the lessor's right to retrieve them. Specialized firms, certified from the department of justice, handle the retrieving procedures in accordance to executive rules.

Article 26

Without prejudice to a more severe penalty contained in another law, the penalty for violations of this Law shall be measured in accordance with the gravity of the violation, with a fine that does not exceed 25% of the leased asset's value, or imprisonment for a period that is less than 3 months, or both; whoever obliterates the data assigned to the leased asset, or changes the asset's characteristics or its descriptions that are registered in the specified record, or sells the leased asset, or sub-leases it without a written consent from the lessor.

CHAPTER FOUR
Final Provisions

Article 27

The Governor, in coordination with the Minister of Justice, shall issue the implementing rules of this law within 90 days of its issuance.

Article 28

This law shall enter into force after 90 days of its publication in the Official Gazette.

IMPLEMENTING REGULATIONS OF THE FINANCIAL LEASE LAW

Article 1

Pursuant to article (1) of the Law, the following words and phrases wherever they appear in this Regulation shall have the corresponding meanings, unless the context otherwise indicates:

Law: the Financial Lease Law.

Regulation: the Implementing Regulation of the Financial Lease Law.

SAMA: the Saudi Arabian Monetary Agency.

Contract: the financial lease contract.

Lessor: a joint stock company licensed to carry out financial lease.

Lessee: a person who owns the benefit of the Leased Asset under the Contract.

Leased Asset: any leasable property, moveable, benefits, services and intangible rights such as intellectual property rights.

Contracts Register: a register for recording financial lease contracts concluded or implemented in the Kingdom of Saudi Arabia, sales contracts ensuing from financial lease, and any amendments thereto in accordance to the provisions of the Law.

Contracts Registration Company: the joint stock company in charge of the registration of the financial lease contracts.

Article 2

In compliance with article (2) of the Law, the Law on Supervision of Finance Companies, and other applicable laws, the financial lease activity shall be considered a professional activity upon fulfillment of the following:

1. Acquiring of Leased Asset by the Lessor shall be for the purpose of leasing to others for financial lease.
2. The aggregate amount of credit granted annually exceeds the amount determined by SAMA.

PART 2: THE CONTRACT

Article 3

The Lessee, upon consent of the Lessor, may assign the Contract to another Lessee, and the Lessor shall document his consent in the property records register within ten (10) working days from the date of assignment. The Lessor's approval must not be unreasonably withheld.

Article 4

The Lessor may assign his rights under the Contract without the consent of the Lessee, unless the Contract stipulates otherwise. Under all circumstances, the following must be fulfilled in the event of assignment:

1. The assignment must not cause detriment to the Lessee.
2. The assignment becomes effective on the date of its registration in the Contracts Register.
3. The assignment does not relieve the Lessor from its obligations under the Contract.
4. If the assignment results in change in the recipient of the lease payments, it shall be enforceable towards the Lessee only from the date of notifying the Lessee of the change.

Article 5

If the Leased Asset needs to be examined by the Lessor, the examination method, time and the person responsible for examination must be set out in the Contract or in one of the attachments thereto, provided that this must not cause detriment to the Lessee or fetter the quiet enjoyment of the Leased Asset.

Article 6

1. The Lessee must forthwith notify the Lessor in writing or by an electronic message, of any events in respect of the Leased Asset that entirely or partially fetter quiet enjoyment thereof, using the contact details set out in the Contract and in accordance with applicable notification rules.
2. The Lessee must forthwith notify the Lessor in writing or by an electronic message, of any events in respect of the Leased Asset that entirely or partially fetter quiet enjoyment thereof, using the contact details set out in the Contract and in accordance with applicable notification rules.

Article 7

1. Where Leased Assets are securitized, in accordance with regulations and rules issued by the Capital Markets Authority, the Lessor remains obligated to forthwith disclose to SAMA any technical, commercial, legal, or other risks in relation to the securitized contract, the underlying asset, or the securitization as a whole.
2. In case of the issuance of securities, the Lessor remains obliged to ensure compliance with all related supervisory requirements.

Article 8

The Lessee may request the necessary licence for possessing, operating, or executing the subject of the Contract based on the registered contract and in accordance with the provisions of the Law, in such case; the license shall include the name of the Lessee holding the Leased Asset.

Article 9

1. If the lessee has the right to own property or promise, the contract must include a payment schedule to determine the fair value of the lease and the value of the right to own property separately, on the condition the periodic payment is not less than any period of the lease contract for the purchase of the asset for that period.
2. Without prejudice to the provisions of paragraph (1) of Article 9 of the law, if the contract is terminated during the lease period with the consent of the parties or by the provisions of the contract or law, the lessee has the right to recover the value of the right to own property for the period paid.
3. The lessee has the right to receive the insurance compensation, if any and required.

Article 10

1. SAMA may establish financial lease contract standards that ensure the integrity of the financial system, fairness of transactions, and achieve the objectives of the Law and its Regulations.
2. SAMA may adopt standard financial lease contracts that take into account the rights of the Lessee.
3. The Lessor must obtain written approval of SAMA on its products before launching it to ensure that their conditions are fair.

Article 11

If a Lessee elects to purchase the Leased Asset under the Contract, at any time, he may exercise the right of early repayment of the Leased Asset upon payment of the remaining installments, and the lessor shall be compensated for the following:

1. Reinvestment cost, not to exceed the cost of term for the following three months
2. The amount paid by the lessor to a third party because the contract of the expenses stipulated in the contract, if such costs cannot be recovered, and that for the remaining period of the contract.

Early ownership may be prohibited, if the subject of the contract is real property and the result of this required deduction of the cost of the term, provided the right is exercised two years after the execution of the contract.

PART 3: CONTRACTS REGISTRY

Article 12

1. Lessors shall establish a joint stock company, or more as deemed appropriate by SAMA, for the purpose of registering financial lease contracts in accordance with the most advanced means and the best practices, enabling secure access to the data in the Contracts Register, and according to the provisions of the Law and this Regulation.
2. Subject to the requirements under the Companies Law, the capital of the Contracts Registration Company shall be determined by SAMA. SAMA may require the founders to provide a study setting out the capital requirements of the company.
3. The ownership of the shares of the Contracts Registration Company shall be divided equally between the Lessors. Later new Lessors shall own shares proportionally with the previous Lessors. Shares of Lessors who lose their licence shall be divided between existing Lessors based on the fair share value of shares at the time of every adjustment. Subject to the provisions of the Companies Law and the Capital Market

Law and its Regulations, the capital of the company may be increased or decreased, by a resolution issued by SAMA, to reflect the entry or withdrawal of the partners.

4. Entry and withdrawal of partners shall be only with the prior written approval of SAMA.

5. Appointment of the Chairman and members of the Board of Directors, senior executives, the head of the Contracts Register, and registrars shall be upon a prior written approval of SAMA, and they may be released from their posts in case of substantial breach of their legal or professional duties by a justified decision by SAMA.

Article 13

The Contracts Registration Company shall distribute its dividends in accordance to the Companies Law after obtaining prior written non-objection of SAMA.

Article 14

The fees for the services of the Contracts Registration Company shall be determined by a resolution issued by SAMA based on a proposal by the Company based on a detailed technical study showing the economic and commercial bases for determining such fees.

Article 15

1. The Contracts Registration Company shall prepare a Contracts Register in accordance with the Law and this Regulation.

2. The Lessor shall register the Contract and any amendments thereto at the Contracts Register within (10) working days from the date of concluding or its amendment. All transactions affecting the contractual rights of the Lessor and the Lessee shall also be registered.

3. The Contracts Registration Company serves to
   a. Register of contracts and amendments thereto.

  b. Register the transfer of the rights of financial lease contracts through securitization transactions.

  c. Disclose Contracts Register particulars to licensed finance companies and competent authorities, with a written consent from the Lessor.

  d. Register ownership contracts resulting from the financial lease contracts.

4. SAMA shall issue a resolution determining the powers of the head of the Contracts Register and the registrars.

Article 16

1. The head and registrar of the Contracts Register shall satisfy the following requirements:

  a. Be a Saudi national.

  b. Have not been convicted of a crime that breaches trust.

  c. Have not been terminated from any prior service by a court ruling or a final disciplinary decision, unless being rehabilitated in accordance to the applicable laws.

Article 17

The contracts registrar shall carry out the following duties:

1. Performing the assigned duties at the location of work except in cases where the head of the Contracts Register permits the contracts registrar to perform his duties at the Lessor's location and at the Lessor's expense.

2. Verifying the identity of the parties or their attorneys-in-fact by examining their national identity cards or residence permits.

3. Verifying the legal competence and capacity of the parties or their attorneys-in-fact to enter into a contract.

Contract registrar shall have an official seal for stamping executed transactions.

Article 18

All documents and representations issued by a Contracts registrar shall be in the Arabic language. A document written in a language other than Arabic may be attested, after being translated by an accredited translator; the original document and the translation, in such case, shall be attested together.

Article 19

The Contracts Registration Company shall keep all files necessary for a record of transactions and classified as determined by SAMA.

Article 20

Electronic means may be utilized and relied upon in registering Contracts. SAMA may determine any other procedures or means for Contracts registration as it deems appropriate and fulfilling of the best practices.

Article 21

The head of the Contracts Register shall be in charge of the registration works on the Register. Application for registration and any amendment thereto shall be submitted to the head of the Contracts Register, who shall refer such to one of the registrars for processing. Registration shall be processed in accordance with the Law and this Regulation. If a registrar refuses to execute, document, or to certify a document, the concerned parties may file a complaint to the Contracts Registration Company, and then to SAMA. In case of refusal they may revert to the competent court.

Article 22

1. For the purposes of this Regulation, the following documents shall be deemed proof of ownership of the Leased Asset:
   a. Real estate title deed
   b. Asset ownership document.

    c. Customs card.

    d. Intellectual property registration certificate.

    e. Purchase invoice.

2. Further documents may be approved as proof of ownership by SAMA, which may determine additional requirements relating to the proof of ownership.

Article 23

To evidence registration of the ownership document, the contracts registrar shall record the registration number and affix the stamp on the original ownership document and the Contract. In case of the documents that cannot be stamped, the registrar shall take the appropriate procedures.

Article 24

The following information shall be included in the Contracts Register:

1. Details of all Contract parties and their attorneys-in-fact, including the full name of the Lessee, identity number, name of the Lessor, contact and license details.

2. Detailed description of the Leased Asset, including its name, serial number, production date and country of origin, as applicable, and the ownership title the asset.

3. Information about the insurance coverage of the Leased Asset, if any.

4. Contract term.

5. Lease payment, its method of calculation, and the method of repayment;

6. Written consent of the parties for disclosure of Contracts Register information.

7. Ownership and possession of the Leased Asset provisions.

Article 25

1. The head of Contracts Register shall issue an official certificate evidencing the contents of the Contracts Register. Such official document shall be called the registered financial lease contract.
2. A registered Financial Lease contract may serve as a writ of enforcement according to paragraph 7 of Article 9 of the Execution Law.

Article 26

Upon securitization of the rights arising out of the Contract, the Lessor must record the number of the approval of the Capital Market Authority on the securitization transaction at the Contracts Register. A copy the approval must be made for any remarks thereon.

Article 27

The Contracts Registry, including all information therein, is the property of SAMA.

Article 28

If SAMA licenses more than one company to register contracts, such companies must take necessary measures, under the supervision of SAMA, to ensure unity of information, exchange of information, protection and maintenance of the Contracts Register information.

Article 29

Records shall be kept in the Contracts Register for a period of no less than ten years after the date of expiration of all obligations under the Contract.

Article 30

Subject to the Law and this Regulation, SAMA shall issue a resolution stipulating procedures for registration in the register, details required for registration, and provisions and procedures for access to the Contracts Register by third parties.

Article 31
The Contract, in the event of extending credit for owning residence by a natural person, shall be governed by the provisions of the Real Estate Finance Law and its Regulations.

Article 32
This Regulation shall come into force from the date in which it was published in the Official Gazette.

REAL ESTATE FINANCE LAW

Royal Decree No. M/258, dated 13/8/1433H(3/7/2012)

Introductory Chapter
Definitions

Article 1 {Definitions}
Whenever they appear in this regulation, the following words and phrases shall be given the meanings herein unless the context otherwise requires.

Law: this Real Estate Finance regulation.
Minister: the Minister of Finance.
Institution: the Saudi Arabian Monetary Agency.
Ministry: the Ministry of Housing.
Real Estate Finance Contract: a beneficiary's installment term housing contract.
Beneficiary: a natural person who is the grantee in a real estate financing contract.
Real estate {financier} funds: commercial banks and finance companies which are licensed to engage in real estate activity.
Consumer: any person who benefits from from the advantages of real estate finance services.
Worthy of support: A natural Saudi Arabian person whose income does not exceed the limit specified from time to time by the Minister and approved by the Council of Ministers.
Housing Associations: The institutions and charities licensed in accordance with applicable regulations which specialize in

the provision of housing for those who are unable to house themselves.

Financial market: consists of the real estate finance contracts concluded between the beneficiary and the real estate financier.

Secondary market: the purchase and sale of the rights of the financier which arise from financial market contracts.

Chapter 1
Supervision and Licensing

Article 2 {General Regulatory Provisions}

Entities which specialize in the extension of credit in the real estate finance sector, shall be subject to the following provisions:

1. Banks engaged in real estate finance shall be allowed to own the homes to be financed in derogation of those provisions of paragraph 5 of Article 10 of the Banking Control Law in accordance with this Law and as governed by the Regulations.
2. Real Estate finance companies shall be licensed in accordance with this Law and the Finance Companies Control Law.
3. The licensing of joint stock companies to engage in real estate finance shall be determined in accordance with market needs. The Public Investment Fund may own shares in such companies and may appoint members of the Board of Directors. Licensed Financiers may also hold shares in the company. A portion of the shares shall be reserved for public subscription in accordance with the provisions of the Capital Markets Law.
4. Licensed cooperative finance companies must obtain insurance coverage from cooperative insurance companies to cover risks in accordance with the rules of this Law and the Finance Companies Control Law.
5. In order to protect the Consumer and the Beneficiary, the issuance of standards and procedures related to real estate finance, and the forms of real estate finance contracts to be

used by the Real Estate Financiers shall be reviewed to ensure compliance with the Law.

6. Data relating to the real estate finance market shall be disseminated in order to regulate and promote the development of real estate financing techniques, including techniques to facilitate the flow of data between the primary and secondary markets.

7. The principles of disclosure of the standards of cost of funding and the way of its calculation shall be determined in order to enable the consumer to compare prices.

Article 3 {Application of Islamic Shari'a}

The Real Estate Financier may engage in the business of real estate finance without prejudice to the provisions of the Islamic Shari'a; as determined by resolutions issued by Shari'a committees referred to in Article 3 of the Finance Companies Control Law, without prejudice the to the stability of the financial system and fair dealings.

Article 4 {Publication of Data}

The Ministry of Trade and Industry and the Ministry of Justice may publish the data related to the activity of the real estate market, in periodicals and according to market needs, as determined by the regulations.

Article 5 {Access to Records}

The parties concerned with the registration of real property (e.g., courts, notaries) shall enable licensed Real Estate Financiers to access and review information contained in the records of the property, as determined in accordance with the Regulations and the Ministry of Justice.

Article 6 {Insurance}

Real Estate Financiers and real estate refinancing companies shall cover the risk of real estate finance through the purchase of insurance through cooperative insurance companies in accordance with the provisions of the regulations.

Article 7 {Credit Reporting}

The Beneficiary shall have a credit report with a licensed credit reporting agency in accordance with the Credit Information Law. His payment history shall be submitted to such agency during the period of credit financing. The regulations shall determine the minimum history required for such report as well as other data required during the funding period.

Chapter 2
Government Support

Article 8 {Real Estate Development Fund Guarantees}

The Real Estate Development Fund shall allocate a portion of its approved budget as guarantees and assistance to support real estate financing. The regulations shall determine the necessary procedures.

Article 9 {Government Guarantees}

The Government guarantees the fulfillment of those financial commitments which arise from the guarantees issued by the Real Estate Development Fund made within the limits of and in accordance with the budget of the Fund to support the financing of real estate.

Article 10 {Tax Incentive}

The Minister may propose a tax incentive to the Council of Ministers for investors in real estate securities.

Chapter 3
Secondary Market for Real Estate

Article 11 {Permitted Refinancing}

Without prejudice to the provisions of Article 3 of this Law; Real Estate Financiers, can refinance through the following:

1. The real estate refinancing companies in accordance with the provisions of the rules and regulations.
2. The issuance of securities in accordance with the provisions of the Capital Markets Law.

Article 12 {Exemption from Fees}

Procedures for the placement of a mortgage in the secondary market for real estate will be exempted from property registration fees.

Chapter 4
Terms of Reference

Article 13 {Dispute Resolution, Penalties for Debt Avoidance}

The competent court shall adjudicate disputes arising from real estate finance contracts, and the penalty established under paragraph 1 of Article 35 of the Finance Companies Control Law shall be imposed on anyone who attempts to avoid payment of his debt.

Article 14 {Implementing Regulations}

The Institution shall prepare implementing regulations to be issued by a decision of the Minister within 90 days of the effective date of this Law.

Article 15 {Effective Date}

This Law shall be published in the Official Gazette and shall come into force 90 days from the date of publication.

Implementing Regulation of the Real Estate Finance Law

Article 1 Definitions
The following words and phrases wherever they appear in this regulation shall have the corresponding meanings, unless the context otherwise indicates:

Law: the Real Estate Finance Law.

Regulation: the Implementing Regulation of the Real Estate Finance Law.

SAMA: the Saudi Arabian Monetary Agency.

PIF: Public Investment Fund.

Governor: the Governor of the Saudi Arabian Monetary Agency.

Real Estate Finance: granting credit to a Borrower for the purpose of owning a residence.

Real Estate Finance Contract: a deferred payment con-tract for owning a residence by the Borrower.

Real Estate Financing Contractual Rights: cash flows, mortgage, collaterals and other rights arising under a Real Estate Finance Contract.

Transfer of Rights: transfer of the right to recover a debt or mortgage or any other right arising from a Real Estate Finance Contract.

The Sector: the real estate finance sector.

Real Estate Finance Company: a company licensed to practice Real Estate Finance activity.

Real estate Financier: commercial banks and real estate financing companies which are licensed to practice real estate finance activity.

Real estate Refinance Company: a joint stock company licensed to practice real estate refinancing activity.

Originator: a Real Estate Finance Company who first concludes a Real Estate Financing Contract.

Borrower: a natural person who obtains Real Estate Finance.

Consumer: every person to whom Real Estate Finance services are directed.

Housing Subsidy: financial or credit subsidy provided by the government, residential associations or others for affordable housing.

Real Estate Housing Finance Subsidized Product: real estate finance housing product supported by a Housing Subsidy provided by Housing Subsidy provider through the Real Estate Finance Company.

Secondary Market: trading of the Real Estate Finance Company's rights resulting from the primary market con-tracts.

Article 2

SAMA, pursuant to Article 2 of the Law, is in charge of regulating the Sector and for that purpose SAMA is empowered to perform the following:

1. License Real Estate Finance Companies to conduct real estate activity under the Law, the Law on the Supervision of Finance Companies and their regulations.
2. Take all actions necessary for maintaining the integrity and stability of the Sector and fairness of its transactions.
3. Take all actions necessary for encouraging fair and effective competition between Real Estate Finance Companies.
4. Draft and issuing regulations, rules and instructions required for the Sector.
5. Take all suitable means for development of the Sector, Saudization and enhancing the employees' efficiency through regulating the obligations of the Real Estate Finance Companies regarding training human resources, improving their skills and enriching their knowledge in the Real Estate Finance industry.

Article 3

The Real Estate Finance Company is not allowed to practice any other real estate activities, including the activities of ownership of residences, real estate marketing, development and real estate valuation. The Real Estate Finance Company may own residences only for financing such for the Consumer, provided that the following conditions are fulfilled, ownership shall be for the purpose of validating of Real Estate Finance Contract, the number of residences shall be limited, and the ownership shall not create non-financing earnings.

Article 4

The Real Estate Finance Company is prohibiting from engaging in any kind of financing except real estate finance.

Article 5

1- The insurance of risks shall be managed in accordance with the provisions of the Cooperative Insurance Companies Regulations, and its implementing regulations and the directives of the Institution.
2- The Real Estate Finance Company shall disclose annually the risks that can be hedged by insurance and how to deal with such risks.

Article 6

In accordance to the provisions Article 4, the Ministry of Commerce, the Ministry of Justice and the Ministry of Housing shall collect data related to the real estate market and publish it on their websites on a regular basis, including both sales and rental statistics

Article 7

To give effect to the provisions of Article 5, parties entrusted with the registration of real estate ownership (such as the courts and notaries, real estate registration and authentication offices) , shall permit licensed real estate financiers access to information listed in property records, according to the following procedures:

1. The Real Estate Financier shall make a written request for to access to information.
2. A copy of the real estate license shall be attached to the request.
3. The custodian of real estate records shall provide the property registration certificate including the following information:

   a- The name of the property owner at the time of the request.
   b- The validity of the ownership deed and title record search results. The certificate provided shall be valid for thirty days from the date of issuance.

4. The custodian of real estate records shall provide the requested information to the Real Estate Financier within a period not to exceed five working days from the date of receipt of the request.

Article 8

The Real Estate Finance Company may engage in real estate refinancing in accordance with Article 11 of the Law through the following practices:

1. Real estate refinancing corporations licensed by SAMA in accordance with the Law and this Regulation.
2. Issuance of securities by securitization of real estate assets in accordance with the Capital Markets Law and Regulations, subject to market conditions and upon the issuance of a decision by the Governor.

PART (2)
REAL ESTATE FINANCE CONTRACT

Article 9

1. A Real Estate Finance Company shall comply with the requirements stipulated in the Law, this Regulation, the Implementing Regulation of the law on the Supervision of Finance Companies, other related finance regulations and the rules and directive issued by SAMA for real estate finance. Real estate finance contracts and products must comply with the Law and these Regulations.
2. SAMA shall adopt standard forms of contract for the real estate finance contracts that take into account the rights of the Borrower.
3. The Real Estate Financier shall obtain a "no objection" letter from the Institution before using any real estate contract.

Article 10

Subject to the provisions of the Implementing Regulation of the Law on the Supervision of Finance Companies, a written or electronic contract shall be concluded between the Real Estate Finance Company and the Borrower containing the following information:

1. Names of the parties of Real Estate Finance Contract and the real estate broker, civil registration number or residence number of the Borrower, their official addresses, means of contact including mobile number and e-mail, if available.
2. The real estate agent, if applicable.
3. The tenure of the Real Estate Finance Contract.
4. The total amount of Real Estate Finance.
5. The term cost, the conditions governing the application of the term cost and, where available, any index or reference rate applicable to the initially agreed term cost, as well as the periods, conditions and procedures for changing the term cost.

6. The annual percentage rate calculated according to the provisions of the Implementing Regulations of the Law on the Supervision of Finance Companies.

7. The total amount payable by the Borrower, calculated at the time the Real Estate Finance Contract is concluded. All the assumptions used in order to calculate that rate must be mentioned.

8. The amount, number and frequency of payments to be made by the Borrower and, the order in which payments will be allocated to different outstanding balances charged at different rates credits for the purposes of reimbursement in the case of fixed credit, but in case of variable credit, the variable costs should include an example range consisting of a primary, lower and higher periodic payment amount.

9. If charges or other amounts are to be paid without capital amortization, a statement showing the periods and conditions for the payment of such amounts.

10. Statement describing the consequences of non-payment or delay of the payment of installments.

11. A warning regarding the consequences of missing payments.

12. The collateral and insurance required.

13. The existence or absence of a right of withdrawal, the period during which that right may be exercised and other conditions governing the exercise thereof.

14. The right of early repayment, the procedure for early repayment, as well as, where applicable, information concerning the Real Estate Finance Company's right to compensation and the way in which that compensation will be determined.

15. The procedure to be followed in exercising the right of termination of the Real Estate Finance Contract.

16. Information of the residence subject-matter of the Real Estate Finance Contract, including the name of the city, district, and street, residence number, type, space, and construction date.

17. The Real Estate Finance Company's acknowledgement of verifying the real estate ownership validity and its absence of any encumbrances and the real estate condition.
18. Adoption of the beneficiary property by previewing and approval, without prejudice to the responsibility of real estate financier in the verification of the integrity of the property
19. Real Estate Finance repayment account number and bank name.
20. The real estate developer's or contractor's warranty period of the building and the name of the building contractor and designer.
21. For real estate properties where ownership is parceled out, the owner's association registration number, date, and place.
22. Examination mechanism of the Real Estate Finance Company to verify the validity of the real estate property at least once every three years.
23. The Borrower's permission to include its details in the credit report.
24. In case of a Real Estate Finance Contract where the term cost is a variable rate, a de- scrimption of the equation that determines the rate shall be included in a way that facilitates the Consumer's understanding of the term cost and the distribution of the cost over the repayment period.
25. Any other data or information as may be required by the Institution.

Article 11

At the top of the real estate contract there must be placed a summary in plain language, in a form approved by the Insitution, which contains basic information describing the product and funding and the basic provisions of the financing contract. The receipt of the summary by the Borrower shall be documented and included in the file.

Article 12

The Real Estate Financier shall not grant a credit facility in excess of 70% of the value of the real estate financed. The Institution has the right to change this ratio in accordance with prevailing market conditions.

Article 13

The Real Estate Finance Company shall verify the validity of the residence title deed, subject-matter of the Real Estate Finance Contract, and ensure its absence of any in - rem rights affecting the Real Estate Finance Company rights. The Real Estate Finance Company shall document in the financing file the confirmation of registering the ownership provided by competent authority.

Article 14

1. The Real Estate Finance Company shall verify the credit report of the Borrower to confirm solvency, repayment capacity and credit conduct of the Borrower. The confirmation of such must be documented in the financing file.
2. The Real Estate Finance Company shall, upon the approval of the Borrower, register the information of the Borrower and the amount of loan at a company, or at more than one company, licensed to collect credit information.
3. The Real Estate Financier shall reject any loan application that is not in compliance with paragraphs (1) and (2) of this Article.

Article 15

In Real Estate Finance Contracts, the credit report of the Borrower shall include Name of the Borrower, identification number, place of residence, current place of work, marital status, academic credentials, personal data, monthly income, and data of the dependents of the Borrower And any other information determined by the institution

Article 16

The real estate contract must permit the right of the Real Estate Financier to transfer or assign all of its rights to third parties in the secondary market without the consent of the Borrower, including the right to mortgage and other guarantees.

PART (3)
REAL ESTATE REFINANCING CORPORATIONS

Article 17

1. The Real Estate Refinancing Corporation and any other real estate refinancing company must be licensed by SAMA to carry out a real estate refinance activity in accordance with this Regulations and the Implementing Regulations of the Law on the Supervision of Finance Companies, subject to the following modifications:
   a- A license will only be granted for a real estate refinancing activity.
   b- The required minimum registered capital for the Real Estate Refinancing Corporation and any other real estate refinancing corporation is SAR 5 billion.
2. The Real Estate Refinancing Corporation and any other corporation licensed to carry out a real estate refinancing activity are subject to the supervision of SAMA in accordance to the Law and these Regulations, the Law on the Supervision of Finance Companies and its regulations and the circulars issued by SAMA.

Article 18

1- The Public Investment Fund, or any entity which is wholly owned by the Public Investment Fund, upon the initial approval of SAMA, may establish a real estate refinancing corporation in the form of a joint stock corporation bearing the name "Saudi Real Estate Refinancing Corporation".

2- The Public Investment Fund may invite shareholders to participate in the ownership of the Real Estate Refinancing Corporation after obtaining the approval of SAMA.

3- Real Estate Finance Companies that satisfy regulatory requirements, and after obtaining the approval of SAMA, may be permitted to acquire equal portions of newly issued shares of the Real Estate Refinancing Corporation at fair market value provided that their aggregate shareholding does not exceed 30% of the total shares of the Real Estate Refinancing Corporation, to be equally distributed among them, on the date on which SAMA determines that the activities of the real estate finance market have achieved stability, or the date falling five years from the date of incorporation of the Real Estate Refinancing Corporation whichever is later.

4- After the conditions set out in subsections 3 of this Article have been met, the Real Estate Refinancing Corporation may, with the prior written approval of SAMA, offer a portion of its shares, by way of a public offering in accordance with the provisions of the Capital Market Law.

5- Fund share must not be less than (51%) of the shares of that company.

Article 19

The purpose of the Real Estate Refinancing Corporation is to establish Secondary Market facilities for trading Real Estate Financing Contractual Rights and to facilitate the flow of funds in order to:

1- Provide stability and growth in the Secondary Market for real estate financing.

2- Provide liquidity to the Secondary Market and provide better access to Real Estate Finance Companies to finance home ownership for real estate Borrowers.

3- Enhance the liquidity of real estate financing in-vestments and ensure good distribution of investment capital available for residential real estate financing between different regions and classes.

4- Function as an intermediary access to local and foreign financing instruments and sources for the real estate financing sector.

Article 20

1- For achievement of its objectives, the Real Estate Refinancing Corporation may:

   a Acquire, hold and manage, dispose of and otherwise deal in any kind of financing obligations and related rights related to residential real estate.

   b Acquire, hold and manage, dispose of and otherwise deal in any kind of financing obligations and related rights related to residential real estate.

   c Issue Sukuk or securities, including real estate covered securities, asset backed securities and any other securities for financing its activities.

2- The Real Estate Refinancing Corporation may impose charges for its services, in order to ensure that all costs and expenses of the operations of the Real Estate Refinancing Corporation are covered by, and fair profits are made from, income derived from such operations so that such operations are financially self-supporting. SAMA is authorized to control and restricts the pricing of such operations by the Real Estate Refinancing Corporation.

Article 21

1. The following rights may be transferred to the Real Estate Refinancing Corporation in the refinancing transactions without the prior consent of the Borrower, debtor or guarantor.

2. After the Real Estate Refinancing Corporation has paid the agreed consideration to a transferring Real Estate Finance Company, such transfer cannot be revoked or otherwise rescinded

in case of an insolvency of the transferor Real Estate Finance Company. The transferred rights do not form part of the Real Estate Finance Company's assets in case of bankruptcy.

Article 22
A Real Estate Finance company has the right to declare an annual dividend upon the decision of its Board of Directors after receiving a no-objection letter from SAMA.

Article 23
1. The Real Estate Refinance Company must insure that the size of the sale and purchase transactions entered into, prices paid and return on investment does not encourage excessive use of their credit facilities.
2. The Real Estate Refinance Company has to avoid excessive use of its credit facilities as this may affect the price of real estate assets in the market.

Article 24
The Real Estate Refinancing Corporation may not:
1. Grant financing to a Real Estate Finance Company using Real Estate Financing Contractual Rights as collateral before such rights have been transferred to the Real Estate Refinancing Corporation as collaterals.
2. Provide real estate financing to Borrowers.
3. Facilitating real estate financing conditions with the objective of affecting housing prices in a way that violates best practices of risk and credit management.

Article 25
The Board will determine the general policies of the Real Estate Refinancing Corporation. Such policies shall come into effect upon non-objection of SAMA.

Article 26

The Real Estate Refinancing Corporation must prepare annual and quarterly reports on the financial condition and operations of the Real Estate Refinancing Corporation, the risks that the Real Estate Refinancing Corporation en-counters and its management plan, and be submitted to SAMA .The reports must include the financial statements compiled in accordance with international accounting standards.

Article 27

No natural or legal person may use the name of the "Saudi Real Estate Refinancing Corporation" or any similar name or reference thereto.

PART (4):
REAL ESTATE HOUSING FINANCE SUBSIDIZED PRODUCT

Article 29

When supporting real estate housing finance product through Real Estate Finance Companies, the Housing Subsidy provider shall prepare a description for each product to assure compliance with policies of credit, risk management, and valid transactions. Such description shall include the following:
1. Eligibility criteria.
2. Subsidy amount.
3. Means of financing.
4. Any other data specified by SAMA according to the type of product.

Article 30

1. The Real Estate Finance Company adheres to all credit rules as determined by SAMA in dealing with the Real Estate Housing

Finance Subsidized Product.

2. The Real Estate Finance Company obtains the written approval of SAMA, prior to providing the Real Estate Housing Finance Subsidized Product to the eligible persons in accordance with the provisions determined by SAMA.

Article 31

The Real Estate Finance Company may only offer Real Estate Housing Finance Subsidized Product, with the contribution of Housing Subsidy providers from the government, residential associations or others, by a resolution issued by its board of directors.

Article 32

This Regulation shall come into force upon enforcement of the Law.

FINANCE COMPANIES CONTROL LAW

Royal Decree No. M/51 dated 13/8/1433H (3/7/2012)

Introductory Chapter

Article 1

Whenever they appear in this law, the following words and phrases shall be given the meanings herein unless the context otherwise requires:

Law: the Finance Companies Control Law

Regulations: the implementation of this Law.

Institution: Saudi Arabian Monetary Agency.

Governor: Governor of the Saudi Arabian Monetary Agency.

Finance Corporation: a joint stock company licensed to practice finance activity.

Beneficiary: a person who is obtaining financing.

Consumer: a person for whom the Finance Companies provides services.

License: the authorization granted by the Institution to a Finance Company to engage in finance activity.

Finance: the extension of credit through contracts for the purposes set forth in this Law.

Chapter 1
General Provisions

Article 2 {Application}

This Law applies to the Finance Companies licensed under this Law.

Article 3 {Islamic Shari'a}

Companies licensed to engage in financial activities under this Law shall act consistent with the provisions of the Islamic Sharia as determined by resolutions issued by Shari'a committees whose members shall be chosen by such companies, and without prejudice to the stability of the financial system and fair dealings.

Article 4 {Licensing Required}

1. Engaging in any of the activities specified under this Law is prohibited except after obtaining a valid license to do so in accordance with the provisions of this Law or other regulations in force.
2. An unauthorized person is prohibited from using any tool to engage in financing activities identified by or reasonably related to the purposes of this Law, whether through documents, papers, declarations or any equivalent word or phrase equals.
3. The Regulations will establish licensing procedures for persons of good moral character to finance goods or services to customers; recognizing the right of the organization to maintain its financial integrity, in order to protect the financial system and the consumer.

Chapter 2
Licensing Provisions

Article 5

First: The founders of a Financing Company or their representatives shall submit a license application to the Institution, which shall contain the following information:

1. Set forth the administrative structure and its operating Laws, and a business plan which demonstrates the technical ability to engage in activity as determined by the Regulations.

2. The company's capital should not be less than the amount required by the Institution and not less than that specified in the Companies Law. Foreign investment shall not exceed the ratio determined by the Institution.

3. Each founding member of the company must meet the following statutory eligibility requirements:

    a He shall not have been in breach of any obligation towards his creditors.

    b He shall not have violated the provisions of the Capital Market Law and its regulations or control Law or banks or insurance companies control Law or collaborative funding Laws.

    c He shall not have been declared bankrupt.

    d He shall not have been convicted of any crime involving dishonesty unless he has been rehabilitated in accordance with regulations, or as determined thereby.

4. Persons who are supervisory and executive candidates for the company must meet the following professional eligibility requirements:

    a) He should have both theoretical and practical knowledge of the finance business

b) He shall not have violated the provisions of the Capital Market Law and its regulations or convicted of violating the banks control Law or the cooperative insurance companies control Law or any other finance Law.

c) He should not have been convicted of any crime involving dishonesty, unless rehabilitated in accordance with the regulations, or as determined thereby.

5. Comply with any requirement as determined by the regulations for the issuance of the license.

Second: Upon receipt of a completed application, the Institution shall within 60 days rule on the application, taking into account market needs, safety and the quality of services.

Third: Upon approval, applications will be forwarded to the Ministry of Commerce to complete the procedures for the establishment and registration of the company in accordance with law.

Fourth: Upon the completion of the establishment of the company and publication in the commercial register, the Institution shall issue a license which shall be valid for five years.

Fifth: A percentage of the ownership of the licensed finance company will be opened for public subscription no less than two years after commencing operations in order to achieve the specified percentage of the profits Law.

Article 6 {Commencement and Suspension of Business Activities}

The Finance Company must commence operations no less than one year from the date of licensing, and may not commence operations after suspending them for a continuous period of three months without the consent of the Institution, and the regulations shall specify the rules governing such procedures.

Article 7 {Cancellation of License}

The Institution has the right to cancel the license if it appears that the Financing Company provided the Institution with false information, or omitted to disclose material information for the purposes of licensing as determined by regulation.

Article 8 {Restricted Shares}

Shares held by the incorporators may not be transferred except with the approval of the Institution, and whoever holds such shares will be subject to the requirements contained in paragraph (3) of the First section of Article 5 of this Law.

Article 9 {Bankruptcy}

The license is terminated if a liquidator is appointed for the Finance Company or the Finance Company is adjudged bankrupt.

Chapter 3
Finance Companies Activities

Article 10 {Activities Permitted}

1. The Institution licenses the Finance Company to engage in one or more of the following types of financing activity:
   a) Real estate finance.
   b) The financing of productive assets.
   c) Financing of small and medium-sized enterprises.
   d) Lease.
   e) Credit card financing.
   f) Consumer finance.
   g) Microfinance.
   h) Any another funding activity approved by the Institution.
   The Finance Company may own assets for the benefit of another person.

The Institution may license enterprises that wish to engage in support activities to Finance Companies in order to promote competition in the provision of these services, and the regulations shall specify the legal form of the enterprise and those conditions which must be satisfied.

Article 11 {Business Activities Prohibited}

The Finance Company is prohibited from the following:

1. Engaging in any other business other than funding.
2. Owning an entity engaged in an activity other than funding, either directly or indirectly.
3. Trading in currencies, gold, precious metals or securities.
4. Trading in real property.
5. Engaging in wholesale or retail trading.
6. Accepting demand deposits.
7. Accepting deposits or non-banking facilities or opening accounts for customers in any form, unless authorized by the Institution, and if so authorized must deposit with the Institution a percentage of the value of deposits to the extent determined by the regulations.
8. Obtain short-term foreign funding without the approval of the Institution, as determined by the regulations.

Article 12 {Financing Activities Prohibited}

1. The Finance Company is prohibited from the following:

    a) Extend any funding without collateral, except where the regulations so provide and determine the extent of and the rules for funding without collateral.
    b) Granting or financing any credit facilities guaranteed by the debtor's shares.

c) Granting or financing any credit facilities to a company - except a joint stock company listed on the Saudi stock market - if one of the members of the Board of Directors or one of the Finance Company auditors is a partner or manager in the firm or company seeking financing.

d) Granting or financing any credit facilities if one of the members of the Board of Directors or one of the Finance Company auditors is a guarantor of the facility.

e) Granting or financing any credit facilities to any member of the Board of Directors, or one of its directors, or their spouses, or one of their relatives to the second degree, except in accordance with the rules specified in the regulations.

f) Granting or financing any credit facilities or guarantee any financial obligation of one of its employees, including payment of salaries for the period specified in the regulations.

g) Owning shares in another Financing Company except with the approval of the Institution.

h) Granting or financing any credit facilities to a company which directly or indirectly acquires an interest in the Finance Company in a ratio exceeding that ratio specified in the Regulations.

i) Granting or financing any credit facilities to a company or on property which the Finance Company acquires directly or indirectly in a ratio exceeding the ratio specified in the Regulations.

2. Without prejudice to any other public or private right as determined by the regulations, each member of the Board of Directors or external auditor who receives received funding in contravention of the provisions of paragraphs (b) or (c) or (d) of paragraph (1) of this Article is considered as a separate violation according to the regulation.

Article 13 {Reserves}

In order to manage potential operating losses, the Finance Company shall establish reserves in accordance with the standards set forth by the regulations.

Article 14 {Issuance of Securities and Debt}

Without prejudice to the provisions of this Chapter, a Finance Company may issue securities and instruments in accordance with the provisions of the Capital Markets Law commensurate with its assets and financial position, as defined by the regulations.

Article 15{Confidentiality}

The Finance Company and its component departments shall maintain the confidentiality of customer data and company operations with respect to its business activities as determined by the regulations.

Chapter 4
Management of Finance Companies

Article 16 {Qualifications of Board Members}

Members of the Board of Directors of a Finance Company shall not:

1. serve on the Board of Directors of any another Finance Company.
2. perform the duties of auditor in addition to membership on the Finance Company's Board of Directors.
3. been adjudged guilty of an offense in the management of a financial institution.
4. have been declared bankrupt.
5. have been adjudged guilty of a crime involving dishonesty unless he has been rehabilitated.

Article 17 {Responsibility of the Board and Executives}

Each of the company's board of directors, general manager and senior executives and branch managers are responsible - all within the limits of his competence – for the violation of the provisions of this Law.

Article 18 {Joint and Several Liability}

Without prejudice to the provisions of paragraph 1(a) of Article 12 of this Law; members of the Board of Directors of the Finance Company are jointly and severally liable for losses resulting from providing financing without collateral.

Article 19 {Review Committee}

Each Finance Company must establish a Review Committee whose members are different from the Board of Directors. The Board will submit to the Finance Company's General Assembly a resolution concerning the Review Committee's duties, rules for the selection of its members and their terms of office.

Article 20 {Disclosure}

The Chairman of the Board and its members and staff of the Finance Company with authority to make financing decisions must make written disclosures of the following:

1. Any relationship with any contracting party.
2. The existence of any contracting party who is a relative to the second degree.
3. The existence of any financial interest, including in anyone who has a relationship to the contract.

In the case of non-disclosure, an aggrieved person may initiate proceedings before the Committee to request revocation of the contract.

Chapter 5
Supervision of Finance Companies

Article 21 {SAMA as Regulator}
The Institution oversees the work of the Finance Companies and exercises its powers under the provisions of this Law and its Regulations.

Article 22 {Matters Regulated}
These rules regulate the following:

1. The upper limit of the total funding, which the Finance Company may offer.
2. Preventing or restricting the Finance Company from entering into certain transactions.
3. Special conditions that the Finance Company must take into account with respect to certain credit ratings.
4. The minimum ratios of collateral required to support the amount financed by guaranteed assets
5. Disclosure to the public of the cost of funding and method of calculation to enable consumers to compare prices.
6. Controls required to protect the fairness of transactions, and the rights of consumers.
7. Principles for the fair distribution of profit for financing on an accrual basis.
8. Finance Companies' conduct with respect to the protection and application of payments made by the Beneficiaries.
9. Debt collection practices and license conditions.
10. Any another matter within the discretion of the Institution in accordance with the provisions of this Law.

Article 23 {Capital Adequacy Ratio}
The Finance Company must adhere to the rules of capital adequacy ratios as determined by the Regulations.

Article 24 {Diversification}

The Finance Company should diversify the risk of its lending activities and it is not permissible to grant funding for a single enterprise or a group of interconnected establishments in an amount which that exceeds the percentage specified in the Regulations.

Article 25 {Acquisitions or Amendment to Capital}

Taking into account the requirements of these Regulations, the approval of the Institution must be obtained to amend the Finance Company's capital or amend its rules or Articles of Association or the acquisition of a similar company.

Article 26 {Opening of Branch Office}

The Finance Company must obtain the approval of the Institution to open a branch, agency or office within or outside the Kingdom, or close any of them.

Article 27 {Appointment of External Auditor}

The Finance Company must appoint one or more external auditors. The Institution may appoint another auditor at the expense of the Finance Company in those circumstances specified by the Regulations.

Article 28 {SAMA Review of Finance Company Records}

The Finance Company shall provide such data as is required by the Institution, and the Institution shall review Finance Company records and accounts on a regular basis, and if the company declines to submit to the examination required by the Institution this shall be considered a violation of the provisions of this Law.

Article 29

Where a Finance Company has engaged in professional irregularities or any transaction has exposed its shareholders or creditors to unwarranted risk, or if the Finance Company's debts exceed its assets, the Institution shall issue a written disciplinary decision commensurate with the nature of the offense, including but not limited to the following:

1. Warning the company.
2. Require implementation of a program to remove the violation and correct the situation.
3. Obliging the Financing Company to cease or reduce the distribution of profits.
4. Impose a fine as stipulated in Article 34 of this Law.
5. Requiring the dismissal or temporary suspension of the non-Board member employee depending on the seriousness of the violation.
6. Suspending the Chairman of the Board of Directors, or any of the members of the Board from work on a temporary basis.
7. Appointing one or more advisors to assist in the management of the business at the Finance Company's expense.
8. Within the discretion of the Institution, suspend the authority of the Board of Directors and assign a new Manager at the expense of the Finance Company to manage its business until the reasons for suspension are eliminated.

If Institution determines that the violation requires revocation of the license or liquidation of the company; it shall bring termination proceedings before the competent court. In its discretion the Institution may suspend the license pending termination of the proceedings.

Article 30 {Appeal}
Any interested party may appeal the decision of the Institution to a competent court within sixty days from the date of receiving communication of the decision.

Chapter 6
Dispute Resolution

Article 31 {Disputes}

The competent court shall consider the disputes arising from applying the provisions of this Regulation and shall apply the sanctions set forth herein.

Article 32 {Examination Staff}

The Governor shall appoint qualified professional staff to undertake the following duties:

1. Examination and supervision work.
2. Investigation of violations of the provisions of this Law.
3. Prosecution before the competent committee.

Regulations specifying procedures governing the implementation of this Article shall be established without prejudice to the provisions of the Criminal Procedure Code.

Article 33 {Early Repayment}

Financing Companies must disclose to customers before entering into financing contracts the terms of early repayment and regulations shall specify the criteria for early repayment formulas to achieve justice between the parties to the contract.

Chapter 7
Sanctions

Article 34 {Fines}

The Institution may impose a fine not exceeding (250,000) two hundred and fifty thousand riyals for committing any of the offenses set forth in article 29 of this Law, and for continuing violations may impose a fine not to exceed (10,000) ten thousand riyals for each day that the offense continues.

Article 35 {Sanctions for Late Payment, General Penalties}

1. Anyone who attempts to delay the payment of his debt shall be fined. The fine shall not exceed twice the amount of profit attributable to the delay. Sanctions will be imposed for repeat violations. The fine shall be deposited deposited in accounts supervised by charitable institutions for the benefit of those charitable institutions.
2. Without prejudice to the requirements of Article 34 of this Law, anyone who violates any of the provisions of this Law and its Regulations will be punished by a fine but not more than (500,000) five hundred thousand riyals and imprisonment for a period not exceeding two years, or both; according to the gravity of the offense.

Chapter 8
Final Provisions

Article 36 {Grandfather Clause}

Existing companies that engage in financing activity in the Kingdom prior to the entry into force of this Law are granted a two-year deadline for the regularization of their status in accordance with the provisions of this Law.

Article 37 {Taxation}

The Department of Zakat and Income Tax issue the necessary criteria for the calculation of zakat for Finance Companies.

Article 38 {Effect on Other Laws}

This Law shall supersede any law inconsistent with its provisions.

Article 39 {Implementing Regulations}

The Governor shall issue regulations within ninety days from the effective date of this law.

Article 40 {Effective Date}

This law will come into force after ninety days from the date of its publication in the Official Gazette.

IMPLEMENTING REGULATIONS OF THE LAW ON SUPERVISION OF FINANCE COMPANIES

PART 1:
Definitions and General Provisions

Article 1 The following words and phrases wherever they appear in this Regulation shall have the corresponding meanings, unless the context otherwise indicates:

Law: the Law on Supervision of Finance Companies.

Finance Laws: the Financial Lease Law, the Real Estate Finance Law, and the Law on Supervision of Finance Companies

Regulation: the Implementing Regulations of the Law on Supervision of Finance Companies.

SAMA: the Saudi Arabian Monetary Agency.

Governor: the Governor of the Saudi Arabian Monetary Agency.

Finance Company: a joint stock company licensed to carry out finance activity.

Borrower: a person receiving finance.

Consumer: a person to whom Finance Company's services are directed.

License: a license issued by SAMA to a joint stock company to carry out finance activity.

"Finance Activity" or "Finance Activities": one or more of the activities listed in Article (10) of the Law or any other finance activities approved by SAMA pursuant to Article (10) of the Law.

Financing: extending credit under contracts for the activities set out in the Law.

Finance Agreement: a contract by which the Finance Company extends credit to the Borrower for the activities set out in the Law.

Installment: the Total Amount Payable by the Borrower minus non-recurring costs or expenses, such as administrative services fees, distributed over the term of the Finance Agreement.

Term Cost: the term cost to the Borrower as a fixed or variable percentage applied on an annual basis to the amount of finance obtained.

Total Cost of Finance to the Borrower: all the costs to be paid by the Borrower under a Finance Agreement other than the principle amount, including Term Cost, administrative services fees, insurance, and any charges required to obtain financing.

Total Amount of Finance: the ceiling or the total amounts made available to the Borrower under a Finance Agreement.

Total Amount Payable by the Borrower: the sum of the Total Amount of Finance and the Total Cost of Finance to the Borrower.

Annual Percentage Rate: the discount rate calculated according to the provisions of Article 81 of these Regulations.

Board: the board of directors of the Finance Company.

Senior Management: the managing director, chief executive officer, general manager, their deputies, the chief financial officer and directors of major departments, in addition to the officers in charge of risk management, internal audit and compliance functions.

Exposure: the value of an asset that is subject to credit risks, such as default risk or downgrade risk.

Large Exposure: Exposure to one borrower of 5% or more of the company's paid in capital funding and reserves.

Qualifying Interest: (5%) or more of the shares or voting rights relating to shares in a Finance Company held directly or indirectly either by one person or by several persons acting in concert.

Article 2

SAMA shall supervise the business of the Finance Companies and specifically shall be responsible for the following:
1. License the activity to be conducted in accordance with the law and regulations.
2. Taking all actions necessary for maintaining the integrity and stability of the finance sector and fairness of its transactions.
3. Encouraging legitimate, fair and effective competition among Finance Companies.
4. Issuing regulations, rules, and instructions required for the finance sector.
5. Taking all suitable means for development of the finance sector, Saudization, and enhancement of employees' efficiency through regulating the obligations of the Finance Companies in Saudization and training of human resources, improving their skills and enriching their knowledge in finance industry.

Article 3

Any legal person engaging in one or more of the Finance Activities specified in Article (10) of the Law, or any other Finance Activity approved by SAMA in accordance with the abovementioned article of the Law, including commercial and residential real estate finance and refinance activities, is subject to the provisions of this Regulation.

PART 2:
FINANCE COMPANIES LICENSING

Article 4

No one is allowed to carry out any Finance Activity without a license from SAMA in accordance with the Law and this Regulation. SAMA may exempt some transactions of some provisions of this Regulation when it deems such transactions not to effect the financial system because of their nature or limited impact.

Article 5

Creation of an installment sales system for the benefit of natural persons to facilitate the sale of goods and services is a goal of these Regulations.

Article 6

The Finance Company may only engage in activities for which it has been licensed and which are permitted by the Finance Laws and their regulations.

Article 7

All founding shareholders of the finance company, or their representative, must apply to SAMA for a License. The application must specify the activities for which a License is requested, and includes the following:

1. Completed application form as required by SAMA.
2. Draft articles of association and byelaws.
3. Description of the organizational structure of the Finance Company showing that all required functions.
4. List of all founding shareholders setting out the number and percentage of shares in the Finance Company that each founding shareholder will own.
5. Fit and proper form for founding shareholders signed by each founding shareholder.

6. Feasibility study identifying target market, services to be provided, business model, and strategy of the Finance Company in addition to a five-year business plan that addresses the Finance Activities for which a License is requested and sets out at least the following:
   a. proposed Finance Activities and products and a marketing plan.
   b. credit policies and procedures.
   c. projected annual revenue and expenses and targeted growth rates, taking into account applicable solvency requirements.
   d. projected startup costs and funding thereof.
   e. projected ongoing financing of operations.
   f. branch offices to be established .
   g. Recruitment and training plan, including the projected number of employees and percentage of Saudi nationals at each department and each organizational level, and the training and qualification programs for employees.
7. Fit and proper form for Board members signed by each candidate for Board membership.
8. Fit and proper form for Senior Management signed by each candidate for a Senior Management position.
9. Unconditional and an irrevocable bank guarantee issued in favor of SAMA by one of the local banks for an amount equivalent to the required minimum capital for the Finance Activity or Activities for which the License is requested. Such bank guarantee must remain valid until the required capital is paid up in full. This guarantee shall be released upon the request of the founding shareholders in the following cases:
   a) Paying up capital in cash.
   b) Withdrawing the license application by the founding shareholders.
   c) Refusing the license application by SAMA.
10. Drafts of proposed agreements with third parties, including agreements with related parties and all service providers.

11. Any other documents and information that SAMA may request.

Article 8

Subject to the requirements under the Companies Law, the minimum paid up capital of the Finance Company is as follows:
1. For a Finance Company carrying out only real estate finance activity: (200,000,000) two hundred million Saudi riyals.
2. For a Finance Company carrying out one Finance Activity or more other than real estate finance and microfinance: (100,000,000) one hundred million Saudi riyals.
3. For a Finance Company carrying out only microfinance activity: (10,000,000) ten million Saudi riyals.

SAMA may stipulate higher or lower capital requirements based on prevailing market conditions and public interest considerations, or if, as deemed by SAMA, the proposed business model, scope and nature of proposed activities, or their geographic reach so requires, taking into consideration the magnitude and nature of risks associated with such activities. Capital must be paid up in full at the establishment of the Finance Company.

Article 9

1. Microfinance activity is limited to the financing of productive activities for the benefit of small business owners and craftsmen and alike, in an amount not to exceed fifty thousand (50,000) riyals. SAMA may raise or lower that amount based on market conditions.
2. Finance companies licensed to practice microfinance activity shall follow SAMA's rules and regulations for this financial activity.

Article 10

1. Each founding shareholder must comply with the shari'a and legal competence requirements, as well as fit and proper requirements prescribed by SAMA. No founding shareholder –

owning either a direct or indirect interest in the Finance Company – may:

a. have been convicted of a material violation of any criminal law, the Banking Control Law, the Capital Market Law, the Law on Supervision of Cooperative Insurance Companies, the Finance Laws, or the regulations of those laws, or any other laws or regulations inside or outside the Kingdom of Saudi Arabia.

b. have been declared bankrupt or entered into a general settlement with any creditor.

c. have been convicted of a breach of trust offence, unless rehabilitated and at least 10 years have passed since the last sanction for this crime has been completed and on condition that SAMA has granted its approval.

d. Have requested to withdraw a license application to carry out Finance Activity in the last two years.

e. Have had a previous application to carry out Finance Activity refused by SAMA during the last five years.

f. Each founding shareholders must be fully solvent. A person is not fully solvent if he is in breach of any of his financial obligations or if there is any fact that reasonably indicates that he cannot reliably be expected to continuously comply with his obligations.

2. In the case of a founding member or owner of a of a significant proportion who does not meet the eligibility or suitability requirements established by SAMA, SAMA has the right at any time to prevent them from exercising the right to vote on resolutions of the finance company, or require that a no-objection letter from SAMA be obtained prior to such vote in order to maintain the integrity of the finance company and the application of the principles of the government and protect the interests of the shareholders of the finance company.

3. A written Nona objection from SAMA is required prior to the acquisition of any shares in a Finance Company that is

not publically traded, and the acquirer of such shares shall be
subject to the provisions of this Article.

4. If a founding member or intends to acquire shares of the finance
   company, shall apply the provisions of this article to all who
   owns a percentage (5%) or more of the capital or voting rights
   in that entity

Article 11

Board members of a Finance Company shall satisfy the following:

1. He must not be a board member in another Finance Company.
2. He must not combine work in supervising Finance Companies
   or auditing their financials and membership in a Board of a
   Finance Company.
3. He must not combine work in supervising Finance Companies
   or auditing their financials and membership in a Board of a
   Finance Company.
4. He must not have been dismissed from a previous job as disciplinary measure.
5. he must not have been convicted of a material violation of any
   criminal law, the Banking Control Law, the Capital Market
   Law, the Law on Supervision of Cooperative Insurance Companies, the Finance Laws, or the regulations of those laws, or
   any other laws or regulations inside or outside the Kingdom of
   Saudi Arabia.
6. he must not have been previously declared bankrupt, or entered
   into a general settlement with any creditor.
7. he must not have been sentenced of a breach of trust offence,
   unless rehabilitated and at least 10 years have passed since
   the last sanction for this crime has been completed and on
   condition that SAMA has approved that.
8. he must be fully solvent. A person is not fully solvent if he is in
   breach of any of his financial obligations or if there is any fact
   that reasonably indicates that he cannot reliably be expected to
   continuously comply with his obligations.

Article 12

Any candidate for a Senior Management position in the Finance Company, such as the managing director, chief executive officer, general manager, chief financial officer, department's managers, and officers in charge of risk management, internal audit, and compliance functions, must:

1. Be permanently resident in the Kingdom of Saudi Arabia.
2. be professionally qualified and must have at least five years of relevant experience.
3. he must not have been dismissed from a previous job as disciplinary measure
4. not have been convicted of a material violation of any criminal law, the Banking Control Law, the Capital Market Law, the Law on Supervision of Cooperative Insurance Companies, the Finance Laws, or the regulations of those laws, or any other laws or regulations inside or outside the Kingdom of Saudi Arabia.
5. not have been declared bankruptcy or entered into a general settlement with any creditor.
6. not have been sentenced of a breach of trust offence, unless rehabilitated and at least 10 years have passed since the last sanction for this crime has been completed and on condition that SAMA has approved that.
7. be fully solvent. A person is not fully solvent if he is in breach of any of his financial obligations or if there is any fact that reasonably indicates that he cannot reliably be expected to continuously comply with his obligations.

Article 13

1. The license application must comply with the requirements set out in the Law and this Regulation. The founding shareholders must provide SAMA with any additional information or documents that SAMA may require within (30) days.

2. The license application must comply with the requirements set out in the Law and this Regulation. The founding shareholders must provide SAMA with any additional information or documents that SAMA may require within (30) days.

3. SAMA will issue a written notice to the applicant after the completing all the requirements specified in paragraph (1) of this Article.

4. Within (60) days from the day on which Sajama has accepted the license application as being complete, SAMA will either grant a preliminary approval or refuse to grant a License, giving its reasons in case of a refusal. The preliminary approval does not constitute a License or approval to practice the Finance Activity.

Article 14

Founding shareholders must establish the Finance Company as a joint stock company within six months of the granting of the preliminary approval and provide SAMA with copies of the Finance Company's commercial registration and byelaws, reflecting the licensed activities in accordance with the preliminary approval. The preliminary approval will expire after six months unless SAMA extends its duration for a maximum of six months.

Article 15

1. Once the company has been established and the applicants have provided proof that capital has been paid in full, that any additional initial funding as set out in the business plan has been provided to the Finance Company and that the company has taken all necessary measures to start carrying out the planned Finance Activities, including the establishment of all necessary personnel, systems, equipment and functions, SAMA will grant a License.

2. SAMA may take all necessary measures, including onsite inspections, to verify that the requirements set out in paragraph (1) of this Article have been met.

Article 16

The License shall set out the Finance Activity or Activities for which it is granted. SAMA may restrict the License to certain geographic area or specific types of Borrowers or impose other conditions. The Finance Company is prohibited from engaging in activities other than those for which it has been licensed or activities that violate the License conditions, and in the following:

1. Company licensed to Exercise in real estate activity cannot exercise financing activities other than real estate finance.
2. Company licensed to Exercise in micro activity cannot exercise financing activities other than micro.
3. Company licensed to Exercise in real estate activity cannot have real estate financing with any variation of funding

Article 17

The License shall be granted for a term of five years and may be renewed based on a request by the Finance Company in accordance with the requirements of this Regulation. The renewal application must be submitted to SAMA at least six months prior to the expiry of the License, including the following:

1. an updated strategy and five-year business plan that sets out at least the following:
   a) a marketing plan taking into account existing and planned products
   b) credit policies and procedures.
   c) projected annual revenue and expenses and targeted growth rates, against the performance of the Finance Company over the past five years, taking into account any modifications to the Company's strategy and business plan.

    d) projected liquidity and solvency ratios against the levels of liquidity and solvency ratios of the past five years, taking into account any modifications to the Company's strategy and business plan.

    e) projected ongoing financing of operations.

    f) branch offices to be established .

    g) current number of employees and the percentage of Saudi nationals thereof at each department and each organizational level.

    h) recruitment and training plan, including the projected number of employees and percentage of Saudi nationals at each department and each organizational level, and the training and qualification programs for employees.

2. The financial charges required for renewing the License.

3. Any other documents and information that SAMA may request.

Article 18

The Finance Company must not cease any of its activities for more than three consecutive months unless SAMA has granted its approval prior to the expiry of the three month period, Such approval shall not affect any obligations on the Finance Company.

Article 19

The Finance Company may apply for an amendment of the License for addition or deletion of some activities or amendment of any term or limitation thereof Amendment application must be based on reasonable justifications and accompanied by any documents, information or studies required by SAMA.

Article 20

1. SAMA may revoke the License upon the request of the Finance Company, taking into account the rights of the creditors and Borrowers and the integrity of the financial system.

2. SAMA may revoke the License with immediate effect if the Finance Company has submitted false information or failed to disclose material information that should have been provided for licensing purposes.
3. If the License is revoked or lapses, the Finance Company must be liquidated. SAMA may appoint a liquidator..

Article 21

If the License is suspended, the Finance Company must cease operations with immediate effect and may only continue operations after obtaining the written approval of SAMA thereupon.

Article 22

1. SAMA may charge the following:
    a) (200,000) two hundred thousand Saudi riyals for issuing the License
    b) (100,000) one hundred thousand Saudi riyals for renewing the License.
    c) (50,000) fifty thousand Saudi riyals for amending the License.
2. Exception to the provisions paragraph (1) of this Article, the fees to meet the issuance of the license Exercise microfinance activity, renovated or modified is (10000) ten thousand riyals.

Article 23

The finance company has to get a letter from the institution includes no objection before or put new financial products or modify products list.

PART 3:
SOLVENCY AND LIQUIDITY

Article 24
The Finance Company shall maintain the required levels of solvency and liquidity in accordance with the requirements, standards, and rules set by SAMA.

Article 25
The Finance Company shall complete the prudential data forms in accordance with the forms, rules, and instructions set forth by SAMA and provide SAMA with those reports in prescribed timing

Article 26
The Finance Company shall not approve or recommend dividends distribution or any other distributions without obtaining a non-objection letter from SAMA. In all cases, the Finance Company shall ensure that the following conditions are met before approving or recommending dividends distribution or any other distributions:
1. The distribution does not cause capital adequacy, solvency, or liquidity to drop below the required levels.
2. The distributions must not exceed the actual net profit for the period.
3. Any other conditions set by SAMA are met.

PART 4:
OWNERSHIP AND ASSETS

Article 27

1. No acquisition or disposal of the following shall be executed by the Finance Company unless it has obtained a non-objection letter from SAMA

2. The Finance Company may not execute any partial or total liquidation of its business or of the Finance Company itself without prior written approval of SAMA.

PART 5:
CORPORATE GOVERNANCE

Article 28
The Finance Company must comply with corporate governance rules issued by SAMA.

Article 29
The Finance Company shall develop and implement a specific code for corporate governance and provide SAMA with a copy of the code after its approval by the Board. The corporate governance code shall at least address the following:
1. Organizational structure.
2. Independence and separation of duties.
3. Roles of the Board, its committees, and the composition and duties of each.
4. Remuneration and compensation policies.
5. Conflict of interest controls.
6. Integrity and transparency controls.
7. Compliance with applicable laws and regulations.
8. Methods for securing confidentiality of information.
9. Fair dealing.
10. Protection of Company's assets.

Article 30
The Board must form specialized committees to expand the scope of its work in the areas requiring special expertise, including at least an audit committee and a risk management and credit committee, and

shall grant those committees the necessary powers to perform their work and monitor their performance.

PART 6:
INTERNAL ORGANIZATION

Article 31

The Finance Company must establish appropriate organizational policies, including manuals and workflow procedures. Those policies must be in writing, they must be kept up to date and they must be communicated to staff in a suitable and timely manner. The organizational policies must include rules for at least the following:

1. the organizational and operational structure, decision making and responsibilities.
2. Prevent credit and operational
3. Financial Management
4. Marketing and Sales
5. Technology and Information Security
6. Customer service and collection
7. Risk management and assessment and treatment, control and disclosure
8. Internal control system
9. Internal Audit
10. Compliance and regulations and instructions related
11. Assign tasks to external service providers
12. Salaries, bonuses and incentives, including the salaries of members of senior management and staff and their motivation and remuneration of the members of the Governing Council and its committees.

Article 32

The Finance Company may not combine an executive function such as financing or hedging and oversight function such as internal auditing or accounting tasks. A separation of functions must be adopted in a manner that ensures the application of the generally accepted policies, procedures, and technical standards, to protect the Finance Company's assets and funds, and avoid fraud and embezzlement.

Article 33

1. The Finance Company's technical facilities and related systems must be adequate according to industry standards for the Finance Company's operational needs, business activities, and risk situation.
2. Information technology systems and the related processes must be designed in a manner that ensures data integrity, availability, authenticity and confidentiality. Information technology systems and the related processes must be assessed in regular intervals in line with industry standards and tested before they are used for the first time and after any changes have been made.
3. There must be a business continuity plan for emergency cases that ensures recovery in an appropriate period of time.

Article 34

All business documents, records and files must be kept in an orderly, transparent and safe manner. They must be kept up to date and complete and retained for at least ten years after the documented activity has ended.

Article 35

A Finance Company must have sufficiently experienced and trained staff for its operational needs, business activities and risk situation. Staff must have the necessary knowledge and experience. The remuneration of staff must be aligned with the Finance Company's risk strategy and must not create conflicting incentives.

Article 36

1. At least (50%) of all employees of the Finance Company must be Saudi nationals when the Finance Company starts operations. The (50%) minimum applies to all departments and organizational levels.
2. The percentage of Saudi nationals of total human employees shall be annually increased by (5%) of all employees the until a minimum of (75%) has been reached. SAMA shall determine the minimum required annual increase thereafter.
3. recruitment of non-Saudis in the Finance Company shall be limited to jobs that require expertise not available in the Saudi labor market. In all cases, the Finance Company must obtain a non-objection letter from SAMA before recruiting any non-Saudi employee based on a justified request by the Finance Company.

PART 7:
OUTSOURCING

Article 37

1. The Board must issue a written policy regulating outsourcing. It must be updated every year. This policy shall include in particular the following:
   a) roles and responsibilities of the Board and Senior Management.
   b) eligibility and qualification criteria for outsourcing provider.
   c) risk identification criteria and risk mitigation measures.
   d) rules for the continuous monitoring and controlling of outsourced activities.
   e) Criteria to identify conflicts of interest, if any, and rules or procedures which ensure safeguarding the interests of

the Finance Company and not putting the interest of the other party over the Company's interest.

   f) Procedures to protect information and maintain confidentiality and privacy.

2. SAMA, the Finance Company, and the external auditor must have the authority to obtain any information or documents related to the work of the outsourcing provider or be examined in the offices of the outsourcing provider.

3. The Finance Company must verify the outsourcing provider's compliance with the applicable laws, regulations, and instructions.

4. Any outsourcing arrangement that, in case of disruption or other default, may have a significant impact on the Finance Company's business, reputation or financial situation (Material Outsourcing) requires prior written Nona objection from SAMA. Material outsourcing may not be subcontracted.

PART 8:
RISK MANGEMENT

Article 38

1. establish a clear written business strategy and a written risk management policy approved and updated annually by the Board. The risk management policy should take into account all relevant types of risks and how to deal with them, taking into consideration all business activities, including activities that have been outsourced. The risk management policy must include analysis for at least the following risks:
   a) credit risk.
   b) market risk.
   c) Term Cost rate risk.
   d) Risk of incompatibility of assets with liabilities.

    e) exchange rate risk.
    f) liquidity risk.
    g) operational risk.
    h) country risk.
    i) legal risk.
    j) technology risk.

2. establish appropriate processes to identify, assess, manage, monitor and communicate risks. These processes must be included in a comprehensive risk management framework that ensures the following:
   a) early and complete identification of risks.
   b) assessment of correlations between risks.
   c) immediate communication to Senior Management and the Board, responsible staff, and where appropriate, the internal audit department.

3. establish a risk management function directly reporting to the audit committee.

Article 39

The Finance Company must prepare a quarterly risk report for discussion by the Board after review by Senior Management. The report must include as a minimum the following:

1. an overview of the risk development and performance of financial positions that incur market price risks, as well as any instances in which the limits have been exceeded.

2. changes to key assumptions or parameters which form the basis of the market price risk assessment procedures.

3. the performance of the financing portfolio by sector, country, risk class and size and collateral category.

4. the extent of limits granted and external credit lines. Large Exposures as defined in Article (53) of this Regulation and other significant Exposures, such as problem loans, must be listed and commented on.

5. where appropriate, a separate analysis of country risks, any instances where limits were exceeded and the reasons thereof, the scale and development of new business, and the development of the Finance Company's risk provisioning.
6. any major financing decisions which deviate from the strategies or policies.

Article 40

The Finance Company must submit a report referred to in Article (39) after being discussed and approved by the Board, along with the decisions made in this regard.

PART 9:
COMPLIANCE

Article 41

The Finance Company must comply with applicable laws, regulations and circulars. It must also take the necessary measures and procedures to avoid breaching them.

Article 42

1. establish the compliance function as an independent department reporting directly to the audit committee.
2. develop a written compliance policy approved by the Board, that sets out the rights, obligations and responsibilities of the compliance department, as well as compliance programs and related processes of the compliance function. The audit committee must ensure the implementation of the compliance policy, evaluate its effectiveness, and propose the necessary amendments to it
3. take the necessary steps to ensure that the compliance policy is adhered to.

Article 43

1. Based on the recommendation of the audit committee, a head of compliance shall be appointed by the Board, after obtaining a prior Nona objection letter from SAMA thereupon.
2. The head of compliance acts independently, and reports only to the audit committee. The head of compliance may not have management roles that conflict with his role.

Article 44

The head of compliance must submit a compliance report to the audit committee and thereafter to the Board for review on quarterly basis at least. The compliance report must identify and assess the main compliance related risks facing the Finance Company, analyses existing processes and procedures and assess their viability and, where necessary, suggest any improvements or changes.

Article 45

The compliance department must have staff and resources commensurate with the business model and size of the Finance Company. Employees must report solely to the head of compliance.

Article 46

The compliance department must ensure compliance with applicable laws and regulations. It has, without limitation, the following tasks:

1. It identifies and deals with all compliance risks and monitors all relevant developments.
2. It analyses new business processes or segments, and it suggests measures to address compliance risks.
3. It must follow a risk abased compliance program and report its findings to the audit committee at least quarterly and where the need arises.

4. In respect of all compliance issues, it collects complaints and formulates written guidance to staff, where necessary.
5. It drafts internal policies and procedures to combat financial crimes, including money laundering and terrorism financing.
6. It monitors compliance with all applicable antimony laundering and antiterrorism financing laws, regulations, and rules
7. It promotes awareness of compliance issues and provides training to employees on compliance related matters.
8. It takes the necessary procedure to inform the competent authorities of violations.

Article 47

The finance company has to but internal policies as measures to fight financial crime, and in particular money laundering and the financing of terrorism, and in the application of standards (KYC) and take the necessary measures to inform the FIU about any suspicious activities or processes.

PART 10:
INTERNAL AUDIT

Article 48

1. The organizational structure of the Finance Company must include an internal audit department reporting directly to the audit committee. The internal audit department shall be independent in performing its duties, and its employees shall not be assigned any other responsibilities.
2. The internal audit department assesses the internal control system and the extent to which all department and employees, comply with the applicable laws, regulations and Finance Company's policies and procedures, whether outsourced or not. The internal audit department must have full and unlimited access

to information and documents, including resolutions of the Board that may be relevant to its functions.

Article 49

The internal audit department shall operate in accordance to a comprehensive audit plan, approved by the audit committee and updated on an annual basis. Major activities and processes, including those related to risk management and compliance, must be audited annually.

Article 50

1. The internal audit department must prepare and submit to audit committee written report on its work at least quarterly. This report must include the scope of the audit, all findings and recommendations. It must also include the measures taken by each department in respect of findings and recommendations and whether there are important results that have not been settled on time and the reasons for their unsettlement.
2. The internal audit department must prepare and submit to the audit committee a written general report on all audits in a financial year, compared with the approved plan and stating any gaps or deviation from the plan, if any. This report shall be submitted within the first quarter following the end of the relevant financial year.

Article 51

Working documents must be kept, showing in a transparent manner the work carried out, as well as findings and recommendations.

PART 11: FINANCING POLICIES AND PROCEDURES
CHAPTER 1: FINANCING POLICIES

Article 52

1. The Finance Company shall define written financing policies setting out rules and procedures for granting finance, including for example classification of credit worthiness, dealing with deteriorating credit quality and nonperforming financings, types of accepted collaterals, methods for calculating their values, monitoring, administration and enforcement of collateral, and risk provisioning.
2. All financing policies and all amendments to policies must be approved by the Board and submitted to SAMA.

CHAPTER 2: EXPOSURE LIMITS

Article 53

Exposure includes the value of all assets that are subject to credit risks, including but not limited to, account balances. debt instruments. Finance Agreements and advances to credit institutions and customers. all commitments or other obligations to extend financing or to make a payment or deliver assets to a third party with a right of recourse against a customer or another third party. all other recourse rights against a customer or third party resulting from the provision of a guarantee or other collateral. shares and participating interests. assets in respect of which the Finance Company is the lessor. and all other actual or contingent payment or reimbursement claims against a customer or a third party which expose the Finance Company to a counterparty risk.

Article 54

1. The aggregate maximum financing offered by a Finance Company shall not exceed five times the capital and reserves for

Finance Companies carrying out real estate finance activity and three times the capital and reserves for Finance Companies carrying out other Finance Activities.

2. SAMA may increase the limit on the aggregate maximum financing offered by a Finance Company to seven times the capital and reserves for Finance Companies carrying out real estate finance activity and five times the capital and reserves for Finance Companies carrying out other Finance Activities, taking into account the financial position of the Finance Company and the finance market conditions.

Article 55

1. The aggregate of Large Exposures must not exceed the paid up capital and reserves of the Finance Company unless the Finance Company has obtained a Nona objection letter from SAMA.

2. The Finance Company may not incur an Exposure to a Borrower of (10%) or more of its paid up capital and reserves or an Exposure to a group of Borrowers where one of them has direct or indirect control over the other members of the group of (25%) or more of its paid up capital and reserves (Large Exposure) unless it has obtained a Nona objection letter from SAMA thereupon.

Article 56

1. Any of the following is a related party for the purposes of this Regulation:
   a) any member of the Board or its committee.
   b) any member of Senior Management.
   c) any person directly or indirectly holding or controlling (5%) or more of the capital or voting rights of the Finance Company, and any entity in which such person directly or

indirectly holds or controls (5%) or more of the entity's capital or voting rights.

d) any person directly or indirectly holding or controlling (5%) or more of any class of debt instruments that give their holders a right to a share of the profits or income of the Finance Company.

e) any entity in which the Finance Company directly or indirectly holds or controls (5%) or more of the shares or interests or voting rights.

f) any ancestor or descendant up to the second degree, or spouse of any of the persons listed in the preceding sub-paragraphs (a) through (c).

2. Without prejudice to the public and private rights prescribed by laws, any Board member of the of the Finance Company or any external auditor who receives financing in breach of any of sections (1(b), (1(c), or (1(d) of Article 12 of the Law, shall be deemed dismissed from the date of receiving financing, and the Finance Agreement in this case shall be deemed void.

CHAPTER 3: FINANCING PROCEDURES

Article 57

1. The Finance Company must verify the credit record of the Consumer to confirm his solvency, repayment capacity and credit conduct. The confirmation of such must be documented in the financing file.

2. The Finance Company must, upon the approval of the Borrower, register the information of the Borrower and the amount of financing at one or more of the companies licensed to collect credit information.

3. The finance company has to rejected the funding request in the event counting obtaining the consent of the consumer or the beneficiary referred to in paragraphs (1) and (2) of this Article.

Article 58

1. Administrative levels for granting credit shall be determined based on the type and amount of finance, and the decision for acceptance or refusal of financing shall be subject to the powers granted for each administrative level.
2. The Finance Company must obtain a Nona objection letter from SAMA before extending any of the following:
   a) Financing to a foreign Borrower that is not a resident in the Kingdom.
   b) Financing in a currency other than the Saudi riyal.

Article 59

1. The finance company to follow the scientific method and standards as measures clear and transparent and written to assess the creditworthiness of demanded funding and ability to repay, according to the best practices in this area, and on the Board of Directors the adoption of these standards procedures and reviewed every two years at least and updated when needed. And on the application of this finance company and procedures before granting funding and documented in the file of funding.
2. Risks related to an Exposure must be evaluated and classified before the financing decision is made. The risk classification must be reviewed at least annually.
3. The Finance Company must define processes for the early detection of risks to signal out financing that show signs of increased risk and develop quantitative and qualitative indicators for the early identification of risks

Article 60

1. The aggregate value of collateral must cover the expected Exposure and be no less than the Total Amount of Finance.
2. All collateral must be enforceable and capable of valuation in order to be acceptable. Collateral must consist in a pledge, a security assignment of assets, or a personal guarantee from a third party. Personal guarantees must be evaluated based on the net assets of the guarantor.
3. The value and legal validity of collateral must be assessed prior to the granting of the financing.
4. If the value of the collateral is dependent to a substantial degree on the financial situation of a third party or fluctuations and conditions of the market, the collateral must be evaluated on a regular basis, and appropriate measures to strengthen those collateral shall be taken when its value decreases. The counter-party risk of the third party must be reviewed as appropriate.
5. Collateral risks and provisions for risk must be decided by the Control Function.

Article 61

Financing must be granted against collateral, unless all of the following requirements applies:

1. The finance amount does not exceed (100,000) one hundred thousand Saudi riyal.
2. The Borrower has no history of default on financings he received in the past five years at least.
3. The Borrower must not be a related party.

Article 62

The Finance Company must make provisions for contingent losses and risks in accordance with International Financial Reporting

Standards. SAMA may require that the Finance Company to make an additional provision or more for contingent losses and risks.

Article 63

1. The Finance Company must define cases in which an Exposure requires special observation (Intensified Financing Management). Exposures in Intensified Financing Management must be reviewed on an ongoing basis to determine whether further actions may be required. There must be clear rules determining when a financing must be transferred to personnel specializing in restructuring, scheduling or winding up.
2. The Finance Company must define criteria for write-downs and loss provisions, including country risk provisioning, taking due account of the International Financial Reporting Standards, and ensure that these are applied consistently.

PART 12: ACCOUNTS AND DEPOSITS

Article 64

Insurance risk financing be in accordance with the provisions of the Cooperative Insurance Companies Control and its implementing regulations as issued by the institution of the Instructions.

PART 12: ACCOUNTS AND DEPOSITS

Article 66

The Finance Company must not accept time deposits or nonbanking credit facilities or similar, or open any type of accounts unless it grants SAMA's prior written approval.

PART 13:
TRADING FINANCIAL INSTRUMENTS

Article 66

Without prejudice to paragraph (3) of Article (11) of the Law, the Finance Company shall not own financial instruments except in the following cases:

1. As part of a customary financing transaction where the purpose of the transaction is to grant financing to a Borrower.
2. to invest cash in hand, provided that it only incurs Exposure to Saudi commercial banks or fixed income securities that are approved by SAMA.
3. to hedge an existing Term Cost risk exposure.
4. to hedge an existing currency risk exposure.

PART 14:
REFINANCING

Article 67

1. In accordance with the provisions of Article (14) of the Law, the Finance Company may issue securities or sukuk only after obtaining a Nona objection letter from SAMA.
2. Finance company cannot dispose of finance assets or rights arising therefrom in any form without obtaining a letter from the institution includes no objection. And required to act in finance assets or rights arising therefrom the lapse of one year and at least one from the date of grant funding associated with the asset to be disposed of.
3. The Finance Company must comply with the rules and circulars issued by SAMA in this regard.

Article 68

The Finance Company may incur debt that is either granted by a foreign lender or granted in a currency other than Saudi Riyal after obtaining the prior written approval of SAMA.

PART 15:
STRUCTURAL CHANGES

Article 69

1. The Finance Company must obtain a Nona objection letter from SAMA before appointing persons in the following:
   a) Membership of the Board and its committees.
   b) Managing director, chief executive officer, general manager, their deputies, and directors of the key departments, or their designees.
   c) Managers of control functions, such as internal audit, risk management and compliance, or their designees.

Article 70

The Finance Company must immediately notify SAMA of:

1. Any retirement of a director or authorized person or revocation of such authorization.
2. Losses exceeding (25%) of the paid up capital and reserves of the Finance Company.

PART 16:
ACCOUNTS

Article 71

The Finance Company must apply International Financial Reporting Standards .

Article 72

1. The Finance Company must provide SAMA with its audited financial statements, auditor's report, and Board of Directors' report at least five business days before its publishing date.
2. The Finance Company must provide SAMA with its interim financial statements and auditor's report at least three business days before its publishing date.

Article 73

Without prejudice to the requirements of other laws, the Finance Company must establish a website and publish its annual financial statements and reports including the following:
1. Statement of financial position
2. Income statement.
3. Cash flows statement.
4. Board of directors' report.

Article 74

1. The Finance Company must obtain a prior Nona objection letter from SAMA before appointing an external auditor. SAMA has the right to require the Finance Company to appoint another auditor if the size and nature of the Company's operation so requires.
2. SAMA may require the Finance Company to replace its external auditor or may appoint another auditor at the expense of the Finance Company in any of the following cases:
   a) If the size and nature of its business so requires
   b) The existing external auditor has committed a breach of professional obligations..
   c) There is reason to believe that the existing external auditor has a conflict of interest.
   d) When necessary for the protection of the financial system or the public interest.

3. The external auditor must report to SAMA immediately all facts of which he obtains knowledge in the course of an audit and which:
    a) might justify the qualification or withholding of the certificate of audit.
    b) jeopardize the existence of the Finance Company.
    c) seriously impair the Finance Company's development,
    d) indicate that the managers have infringed any applicable laws, regulations or the byelaws of the Finance Company.
    e) Terminate the contract before the end of the reasons that led to it.
4. SAMA may require the external auditor to explain his report or to reveal other facts that may have come to his attention during the audit and which suggest any violation of a law, a regulation or the byelaws of the Finance Company.

Article 75

1. The Finance Company, its Board members, and employees must provide all information or documentation concerning the Finance Company, its business, its shareholders, and its personnel, that SAMA may request at any point in time.
2. SAMA has the right to inspect the records and accounts of the Finance Company, through SAMA's personnel or by auditors appointed by SAMA, provided that the inspection shall be at the Finance Company's premises.
3. The Finance Company and its employees shall facilitate the task of whom SAMA appointed for inspection and cooperate with them particularly as follows:
    a) Provide the inspector with the Finance Company's records, accounts, and documents that he deems necessary to perform his task.
    b) Provide information and explanations as required by the inspector.

c) Disclose any violations or irregularities in the Finance Company's operations to the inspector at the start of his mission.

d) Adhere to the recommendations and instructions given by SAMA to the Finance Company to address the observations that are uncovered through the inspection's rounds.

4. The Finance Company and any of its employees are prohibited from hiding or attempting to hide any information or irregularities or failing to provide any clarifications requested by the appointed inspector.

5. SAMA's employees in charge of the supervision, control, and inspection shall not be vulnerable to any claims as a result of their conduct to perform their duties.

Article 76

1. Professional violations related abuses referred to in Article 29 of the longer each violation of a provision of the regulation or noncompliance with any of the rules or instructions issued by the institution.

2. From the Irregularities related to transactions was the finance company's shareholders or creditors of the danger referred to in Article 29 of the following:

a) A material adverse change in the activities of the finance company or its financial position or formal or administrative or would threaten its survival or its ability to meet their debts when they fall due.

b) loss of finance company half of the paid-up capital

c) loss of finance company exceeds (10%) of its paid-up capital in each year during the four consecutive fiscal years at least

Article 77

The Finance Company must reimburse all costs of a third party appointed by SAMA as a consequence of measures taken under this Part.

PART 18:
CONSUMER PROTECTION IN FINANCIAL SERVICES

Article 78

Finance Agreements must be drawn up on paper or electronically. Each contracting party must receive a copy of the Finance Agreement and must specify the following in a clear and concise manner:

1. Names of the parties of Finance Agreement, their official addresses, means of contact including telephone and mobile numbers and emails, if available and the National identity number or a Nona Saudi Imam number or commercial registration number of the beneficiary.
2. Type of finance
3. Term of the Finance Agreement
4. Total Amount of Finance
5. Conditions to drawdown.
6. Describe the equation determining the price of variable rate financing contracts cost term to enable the consumer to understand the cost of term, and the distribution cost of the degree of fulfillment.
7. Term Cost, the conditions governing the application of the Term Cost and any index or reference rate applicable to the initially agreed Term Cost, as well as the periods, conditions and procedures for changing the Term Cost.
8. Effective Annual Term Cost.
9. Total Amount Payable by the Borrower, calculated at the time the Finance Agreement is concluded. all the assumptions used in order to calculate that amount must be mentioned.

10. The amount of the amount of premiums in which the beneficiary has to pay and the number and duration, and the style of a breakdown on the remaining funds if the cost of the fixed term, and if cost term variable answers put three examples of the amount of the premiums, taking into account the cost of term and two terms in which highest and lowest.
11. Administrative services fees
12. Periods of payment of money or fees that need to be repaid without payment of the amount of funding, and the terms of that repayment
13. Statement of implications of the delay in the performance of premiums
14. Where applicable, notarial fees
15. Collateral and insurance required.
16. The account number of depositing Premiums and the name of the bank financing
17. Right of withdrawal and its procedures
18. Right of early repayment, its procedures and the discount equation in case of early repayment.
19. Procedures for handling the safety in case of deceasing.
20. Procedure to be followed in exercising the right of termination of the Finance Agreement.
21. Permit the beneficiary include his information in credit record.
22. Any data or other information determined by the institution

Article 79

Financing contract must be at the top of summary contains basic information of the product and the basic provisions of the financing contract, in plain language to the beneficiary, according to the form prescribed by the institution, and documenting the receipt of the beneficiary to the Pitch in funding file

Article 80

If permitted by Finance Agreement, the Finance Company must inform the Borrower in writing of any change in the Term Cost before the change enters into force. The Finance Company must also inform the Borrower, via the official addresses agreed upon on the Finance Agreement, of the amount of Installments to be paid under the new Term Cost and the details concerning the number of Installments or their dates if changed.

Article 81

1. The rate ratio annual is the discount rate and you are the present value of all premiums and other payments owed by the beneficiary, which represents the total amount owed paid by the beneficiary, equal to the present value of payments the amount of funding available to the beneficiary, in the date on which the amount of funding or the first batch of it available to the beneficiary, calculated according to the following equation:

$$\sum_{d=1}^{m} C_d (1+X)^{-S_d} = \sum_{p=1}^{n} B_p (1+X)^{-t_p}$$

   where:

   m: Order of the last payment made available to the borrower of the conversion amount.

   d: order of the Installment made available to the borrower of the conversion amount

   C_d: Installment value (d), which is made available to the borrower of the conversion amount

   S_d: Between the date on which the amount of funding or the first batch of it available to the borrower and the payment date (d) measured in years and parts of the year, so that this period for the first batch received by the beneficiary of the amount of funding zero

   n: Order of the last payment due by the borrower

p: Order of the payment due by the borrower

B_p: Order of the payment due by the borrower

t_p: the difference between the date on which the amount of funding or the first tranche is available to the borrower and the value date of the payment (p) by the borrower, calculated in years and parts of a year

X: The annual percentage rate

2. For the purpose of calculating the annual percentage rate, calculated the periods between the date on which the amount of funding or the first batch of it available to the borrower and the date of each payment made available to the borrower calculated on the basis of a 365 day year.

3. For the purpose of calculating the annual percentage rate, the amount owed is determined by calculating the amount lent to the borrower, including all fees, commissions and costs charged to him, with the exclusion of costs or fees that are due to the breach by the financing company of any of its obligations in the financing contract.

4. Percentage rate must be calculated assuming annual validity of the financing contract for the agreed period and the commitment of the parties of their obligations in accordance with the conditions contained in the financing contract.

5. Subject to the provisions in paragraph 10 of Article 87 of these Regulations, if the contract of funding authorizes a change in the cost of term or fees are included in the percentage rate annual are improperly selected when calculating the annual percentage rate, this rate must be calculated assuming that the cost of term and other fees remain constant throughout the term of the financing contract

6. Calculating the annual percentage rate and disclosed as a percentage with two basis points at a minimum, and forced half a basis point more to a full point

Article 82

The finance company shall use the decreasing balance method in the distribution of the cost of term proportionally between the premiums on the basis of the value of the balance of the amount of funding at the beginning of the period and at the time of calculation.

Article 83

Fees and commissions and administrative costs of services charged by the financing company may not exceed (1%) of the amount of funding or (50000) five thousand riyals, whichever is less.

Article 84

1. The borrower may accelerate payment of the remaining funded amount at any time without being charged the term cost for the remaining period, though the finance company may obtain compensation for the following:
    a) Reinvestment cost, not to exceed the cost of term for the three months following the payment, calculated on a declining balance basis
    b) Whatever the finance company has paid to a third party because of the financing contract as stipulated by the contract, based on the declining balance.
2. As an exception to the provisions of paragraph (1) of this Article, a real estate finance contract may stipulate a period where early repayment is prohibited, provided it does not exceed a ban of two years from the date of execution of a mortgage contract

Article 85

1. In the event of assignment to a third party of the Finance Company's rights under a Finance Agreement or the Finance

Agreement itself or issuance of securities against the rights arising out of the Finance Agreement, the Borrower is entitled to use against the assignee any defense available to him against the original Finance Company.

2. The Borrower must be informed, by means agreed in the Finance Agreement, of the assignment referred to in paragraph (1) of this Article except where the original Finance Company, by agreement with the assignee, continues to service the finance vis-Ã -vis the Borrower

Article 86

1. The Finance Company shall indicate in all product advertisements its name, logo, any identifying representation and contact details

2. Advertisement shall disclose, in a manner that is clear to the Consumer, the name of the advertised product and Effective Annual Term Cost of the product

3. The Finance Company may not do any of the following:
   a) Provide an advertisement that includes an offer, a statement, or a false claim expressed in terms that would directly or indirectly lead to deceiving or misleading the Consumer
   b) Provide an advertisement that includes the unlawful use of a logo, a distinctive mark, or a counterfeit mark

4. SAMA may oblige any Finance Company that does not abide by the provisions of this Article to withdraw the advertisement within one working day of SAMA notice.

Article 87

The Finance Company shall establish a function for complaints handling, designate staff for complaints handling, and put in place clear procedures for receiving, registering, studying, and responding to Borrowers' complaints within a period not exceeding (10) business days. All necessary details of Borrowers' complaints and actions taken thereon shall be entered in a complaints registry.

Article 88:
1. The finance company and its employees to maintain a range confidentiality of clients and their operations and nondisclosure or exposed to other parties except as required by instructions and regulations in the relevant.
2. Finance company employees are prohibited from disclosing any information about the company's customers and operations, obtained through their work, even after leaving the job in the finance company, as they are prohibited from retaining any of this information after leaving work.
3. The finance company has to take the necessary measures to ensure the preservation of confidentiality of clients' information and operations

PART 19: FINANCE SUPPORT COMPANIES

Article 89
No one other than licensed Finance Companies shall carry out finance support activity or more, such as marketing of finance products or collection, except after obtaining a license in accordance with the rules issued by SAMA in this regard.

Article 90
The Finance Company shall not contract or otherwise deal with providers of finance support activities that are not licensed by SAMA.

Article 91

1. The provisions of this part shall apply to violations and cases of public rights arising out of implementation of the Law on Supervision of Finance Companies, and this Regulation
2. Anything not stipulated herein shall be subject to the Criminal Procedures Law, the Law for Prosecution and General Procurement Authority and the general rules applicable in the Kingdom

Part 20: CONTROL PROCEDURES; INVESTIGATION AND PROSECUTION

Article 92

SAMA's officers who are in charge of preliminary determination, investigation and prosecution shall:

1. be Saudi nationals
2. be of good conduct.
3. have not been sentenced of a breach of trust offence or a crime involving moral turpitude, unless rehabilitated.
4. hold a bachelor degree in Sharia or law
5. have passed the professional examination approved by SAMA.

Article 93

1. The preliminary determination, investigation and prosecution staff shall have the power to search for violators, seize materials connected with violations, receive notices for filing cases, collect information and evidences necessary for investigation, and arraign.
2. The preliminary determination, investigation and prosecution staff may seek assistance from criminal investigation personnel when necessary

3. The preliminary determination, investigation and prosecution staff shall not practice supervision and control over Finance Companies.

4. The preliminary determination, investigation and prosecution staff may seek assistance of individuals and companies when conducting their survey, examination, seizing materials connected with violations. The duty of such individuals and companies shall be confined to showing places and materials that requires search and capturing during investigation.

Article 94
The preliminary determination, investigation and prosecution staff and law enforcement personnel and expert assisting them shall not disclose the confidential information, which they come across in the course of their work even after quitting the service.

Article 95
Criminal cases shall be referred to the Committee for Settlement of Finance Violations and Disputes by the Governor or his deputy.

Article 96
SAMA shall refer crimes and violations that are not within its competence to the body concerned with investigation and prosecution.

Part 21: FINAL PROVISIONS

Article 97
Companies and establishments conducting finance business in the Kingdom of Saudi Arabia before the Law enters into force, must provide SAMA within the first six months of period referred to in

Article (36) of the Law with their plan to comply with the provisions of the Law or a plan to exist the market

Article 98
Commission or more will constitute by the decision of the governor to submit proposals and recommendations for the development of the finance sector.

Article 99
Instructions for the implementation of regulatory and supervisory requirements of the finance sector shall be issued by a resolution of the Governor.

Article 100
This Regulation comes into effect upon the enforcement of the Law.

EXECUTION LAW

(Royal Decree No. M/53 dated 13/8/1433 H)

Article 1 [Definitions]

Whenever they appear in this law, the following words and phrases shall be given the meanings herein unless the context otherwise requires:

Law: This Execution law

Regulation: Regulations of this law

Minister: The Minister of Justice

Execution Judge: Head of the Execution Department and its judges, an Execution Department judge, and the judge of the court who specializes in the tasks of execution according to the case.

The President: The President of the Execution Department, an Execution Department judge, or a judge of the court who specializes in execution matters according to the case.

Execution Officer: An individual who is in charge of implementing execution procedures according to the provisions of the law.

Process Server: A court officer, who may act at the behest of the plaintiff in execution, or a person licensed by the Ministry of justice to serve court announcements, appointments , orders , and other judicial documents required by law.

Agent of Judicial Sale: A person who is licensed by the Ministry of the Justice to sell the debtor's property in order to pay the Creditor.

Decisions: Procedures of the Execution Court, its orders excepts rulings in disputes.

Contentious Executions: Lawsuits that arise relating to the validity of execution, and litigated by parties which dispute an execution.

Part One
Chapter One
OFFICE OF THE EXECUTION JUDGE

Article 2 [Authority of Execution Judge]

Except for matters relating to the conduct of administrative criminal cases, the Execution Judge has the authority to order compulsory execution and supervision. He is assisted by execution officers. He may issue judgment within his jurisdiction, unless the law provides otherwise.

Article 3 [Jurisdiction]

The Execution Judge shall adjudicate any execution dispute regardless of value. In order to dispense swift justice, he shall have jurisdiction to issue orders in aid of execution, and has jurisdiction to use the police or lawful force, to issue a travel ban as well as to order imprisonment and release, force a debtor to disclose assets, and issue orders relating to insolvency.

Article 4 [Venue]

The venue of execution matters in each case is as follows:

1. The jurisdiction of the Court that issued the executive bond.
2. The region of the debtor's upbringing.
3. The debtor's residence.
4. The home country of the debtor, or the place where movable property is found.

   Regulations in implementation of this Article will issue.

Article 5 [Multiple Proceedings]

In the case of multiple requests for execution, the Execution Judge who has issued the first order has the responsibility to supervise the execution, and distribution of funds. He may delegate authority to another Execution Judge in another department with respect to the execution of a debtor's assets.

Regulations in implementation of this Article will issue.

Article 6 [Finality of Orders]

Decisions of the Execution Judge are final orders, and as such, all orders and decisions in implementation of execution and insolvency proceedings are subject to appeal. The ruling of the appellate court shall be final.

Article 7 [Obstruction of Justice, Break Orders]

If there is an assault, resistance, or an attempt to disrupt enforcement, the execution judge shall take all precautionary measures, and has the authority to ask the competent authorities to provide necessary assistance. However, it is not permissible for executing officers to break down doors, or force open locks except under an order signed by the execution judge. The order shall be made part of the record.

Chapter Two: The Execution Order

Article 8 [General]

1. The Execution Department is a division of the public court with responsibility for its own procedures and their implementation, and may create more than one branch when needed.
2. The individual judge of the public court has responsibility for implementation of the execution procedures.

3. The Supreme Judicial Council has the authority to create specialized courts for enforcement and execution of judgments,
   orders and letters rogatory from a judge or other authority, as
   needed.

Article 9 [Compulsory Enforcement]

Compulsory enforcement is not permissible save under an executive order in an amount certain as determined. Orders which may be
the subject of an execution are as follows:

1. Judgments, decisions, and orders issued by the courts
2. Provisions of arbitrators appended with order of enforcement
   in accordance with the rules of arbitration.
3. Records of settlement issued by authorized entities or ratified
   by the courts.
4. Commercial contracts.
5. Documented contracts and official notes.
6. Provisions, court orders, the decisions of arbitrators, and letters
   rogatory issued in a foreign country.
7. Regular recognized documents the contents of which are admitted in whole or in part.
8. Self-executing contracts and other papers which have the force
   of the execution order under the rules.

Article 10 [Execution and Permissible Objections]

Judgments shall not be forcibly executed unless final and the
time for appeal has expired unless they are covered by summary
execution, or where summary execution is provided for in the relevant
regulations.

Article 11 [Treaties and International Agreements]

With respect to the requirements of international treaties and
agreements; a judge may not order the execution of a foreign judg-

ment or order except on the basis of reciprocity and after verification of the following:

1. That the courts of the Kingdom are not competent to hear the dispute in which the judgment or order had been issued, and that foreign courts which issued it are competent to do so in accordance with the rules of international jurisdiction prescribed in the regulations.
2. That the litigants in the case where the judgment issued attended, litigated and were afforded due process of law and an opportunity to defend themselves.
3. That the judgment or order has become final and in accordance with the system of the court that issued it.
4. That the judgment or order does not conflict with a judgment or order issued before on the same subject of a competent judicial authority in the kingdom.
5. The judgment or order does not violate the provisions of public order in the Kingdom.

Article 12 [Arbitration]
The provisions of the preceding Article shall apply to the orders of an abitral body issued in a foreign country.

Article 13 [Letters Rogatory]
Judgments obtained in a foreign country may be enforced on the same terms and conditions established by the regulations of Saudi Arabia for the enforcement of judicial orders issued in the Kingdom and on the basis of reciprocity.

Article 14 [Validity of Orders and Orders issued in a Foreign Country]
Judgments, orders and letters rogatory issued in a foreign country shall be submitted to the competent judge for the execution of foreign judgments in order to verify that the order meets the legal

requirements for execution, and if so, to approve execution and show same by placing a seal on the order sought to be enforced.

Article 15 [Proof]

1. If the debtor confesses the debt in writing, the Execution Judge must approve the confession and said approved confession will constitute the execution order.
2. If the debtor disputes the debt, the Execution Judge may examine the objection under penalty of punishment set forth in this law, and this examination when reduced to writing will be considered an execution order if the debtor fails to object. In case of objection, the creditor has the right to litigate the matter before the court having jurisdiction.

Chapter Three: Disclosure of Property

Article 16 [Discovery, Ex-Parte Garnishment]

The Execution Judge shall order disclosure of the debtor's funds in an amount that will meet the amount of the debt, and the order of disclosure and execution may issue after informing the debtor of the order of execution. However, if it appears to the Execution Judge that the debtor, based on his credit report, has a history of delaying payment, he may order disclosure and garnish any funds so discovered without notifying the debtor.

Article 17 [Report of Assets]

Within a period a period not exceeding (20) days from the date of notifying the competent authorities, agencies or entities holding funds owed to the debtor, the debtor, his accountant, his lawyer and staff must disclose all of the debtor's assets pursuant to an order issued by an Execution Judge.

Article 18 [Creation of Departments within Government Agencies and the Private Sector]

All competent authorities or supervising the registration money must implement the following:

1. Create competent departments to deal with orders of execution.
2. Create property ownership databases, to cover real property, financial, property relating to a trade or business, intellectual property or any other assets.
3. Officers and employees of these departments must maintain the confidentiality of the data and information known to them because of their work and not to disclose it to third parties for any reason whatsoever.
4. Implement technical mechanisms to insure only authorized access to data.
5. Notwithstanding any other provision of law, advise the owners of the property of authorized disclosures after a period specified in the Regulations.

Article 19 [Reciprocity]

An Execution Judge may order disclosure to other countries on the basis of reciprocity except where such disclosure does not comply with requirements of the regulations and decisions of the Council of Ministers or where the national security of the Kingdom might be affected.

Chapter 4: Property Subject to Execution

Article 20 [Debtor's Property Guarantee for Debts]

The debtor's funds shall serve as a guarantee for his debts. Any transaction involving the debtor's seized funds shall not be effective.

Article 21 [Property Exempt from Execution]
The following are exempt from garnishment and execution:

1. State-owned property.
2. House inhabited by the debtor and his or her dependents legally, as determined by the judge, unless the property is subject to a mortgage.
3. A vehicle owned by the debtor and his or her dependents legally, unless the vehicle is subject to a security interest.
4. Wages and salaries except for the following:
   a. Half of the total wage or salary for family support
   b. One-third of the total wage or salary for other debt

   Where these are ovelapping, half of the total wage or salary will be allocated for family support and one-third of the other half for other debts.

   In case of multiple debts, the third of the half shall be divided amongst creditors according to the shari'a and the law.
5. The tools the debtor needs in order to practice his profession.
6. The personal effects of the debtor after a determination by the judge as to amount.

Article 22 [Deposits in lieu of Attachment]

1- The garnishee is allowed, according to the the garnishment procedures, to deposit an amount of money that satisfies the debt into the registry of the court which shall be used only to satisfy the debt. This deposit will result in the removal of the lien on the garnished amount in favor of sums in the court registry.
2- Garnishment may only be had on the amount of the claimed debt, unless the asset garnished is indivisible.
3- The Execution Judge is to order the distribution of the garnished amount in order to achieve prompt resolution.

Chapter 2
Preemptive Seizure

Article 23 [Generally]

The court having jurisdiction over the dispute shall be responsible and shall establish procedures for pre-emptive seizure, according to the provisions of summary justice.

Article 24 [Movable Assets]

Creditors have the right to demand preemptive seizure of the debtor's movable assets in the event the debtor does not possess a fixed residence in the kingdom, or in case the creditor fears, based on good cause, the concealment or dissipation of the debtor's money.

Article 25 [Landlord and Tenant]

Lessors of real property have the right to demand preemptive seizure of movable assets, or on the fruits of leased land, as a guarantee for accrued rent.

Article 26 [Petitory Actions]

A person who claims ownership of moveable property has the right to demand preemptive seizure against the person in possession of the property where there is clear proof that support his claim.

Article 27 [Availability of Relief]

A creditor with a debt certain, even if he has no judgment, has the right to request preemptive seizure of the debtor's property in the hands of others, even if the debt is deferred or conditional or on movable property. The custodian of such property which is the subject of a seizure has ten days from the date of notice of seizure to disclose that property which is in his possession. He shall then deposit into the registry of the Court sums sufficient to satisfy the debt within ten days of receiving notice of the seizure.

Article 28 [Need for Clear Right]

Preemptive seizure in the absence of a judgment is not permitted except in the case of a clear right.

Article 29 [Court Order Required]

Seizure is not permitted in the cases set forth in the previous articles except by a court order upon consideration of evidence held by the court having jurisdiction and proper venue. A court may not issue a seizure order before a review of the evidence supporting the seizure.]

Article 30 [Power of Court to Enter Prejudgment Seizure]

A court having jurisdiction of the underlying dispute has jurisdiction to enter a preemptive seizure order.

Article 31 [Notice and Need to Commence Action]

A creditor who has obtained a seizure order must notify the debtor and the custodian of the property within ten days or the seizure order will be null and void. The creditor must initiate a lawsuit to recover a debt within ten days after receiving a seizure order or the seizure order will be null and void.

Article 32 [Bond]

A creditor who applies for a seizure order must provide the Court with a written undertaking indemnifying the custodian if it later is found that the seizure was unfounded and resulted in damages.

Article 33 [Applicability of Procedures]

Property seized preemptively is subject to these rules except those having to do with the sale of any assets seized.

Part III
Execution Procedures

Chapter One
Execution

Article 34 [Contents of the Application]

1. Executions will issue upon the petition of the Creditor on the form specified in the Implementing Regulations.

2. (a) The Execution Judge will verify that the completed execution form is attached to the Execution Order as provided for in paragraphs 1-3 of Article 9 of this law.

   (b) Except for those matters covered in paragraph 2(a) of this Article, the Execution Judge will review the legal sufficiency of the documents submitted under paragraphs 4-8 of Article 9 of this law. If the submission is otherwise in order, he will affix his Execution seal containing the word "Execution Document" followed by the name of the Execution Judge, the division of his court and his signature.

3. The Execution Judge will then immediately issue an Order of Execution to the Debtor with a copy of the Execution Report which must bear the seal of the court and be prepared in accordance with the same formalities as the original. The Order of Execution must be served on the Debtor in accordance with the regulations. If service is not effected within 20 days from the issuance of the Order, the Order of Execution must be published in a newspaper of general circulation located where the court sits with the costs of publication charged to the Debtor.

4. The Ministry of Justice will coordinate with the relevant authorities in order to obtain the address of persons whose residence is unknown.

Article 35 [Execution on Movable Property]

1. The Execution Officer effects seizure of the asset by visiting the place where the asset is located or issuing a written order to the competent authorities to seize the asset in accordance with the rule of the case. The Execution Officer must file a report on the seizure and must sign the asset log.
2. If a seizure is not completed in one day it may take as many days as are necessary including holidays.
3. Release of the asset may not be granted except on order from the Execution Judge.

Article 36 [Valuation of Property]

1. Where the Debtor and Creditor do not agree on the value of an asset, an assistant judge may accompany a specialized legal estimator who is expert in the valuation of assets in order to estimate the value. The legal estimator's opinion will be attached to the seizure report and shall bear his signature.
2. If the valuation of an asset requires entrance upon property, the estimator shall be accompanied by the police. The Execution Judge may authorize the use of force if the Debtor refuses to permit access or is absent.

Article 37 [Deposit of Valuables]

The Execution Officer shall deposit monies, jewelry antiques and other valuable items into the registry of the court subject to the discretion of the Execution Judge according to the requirements of each case.

Article 38 [Safeguarding Seized Assets]

The Execution Officer may secure the seized asset if necessary. He must put locks and the court seal on such asset and detail these actions in the report filed with the court.

Article 39 [Crops]

Fruits and crops may be seized prior to harvest. The Execution Officer shall place a banner at the entrance to the field and affix to it a Notice of Seizure. Land may be sold after the crops mature.

Article 40 [Travel Bans]

A travel ban order shall be composed according to regulations and shall include the following:

1 Identification of the defendant.
2 Identification of the Execution Order, including its number, date and issuing court.
3 An estimate of the asset seized, its description , its amount, weight, type, number, and specific characteristics related to value.
4 Type of the act of ownership of the real property , its number, identification, location, boundaries and area.
5 The value of the seized asset according to the official estimate.
6 The location of the seized property.
7 The name of the custodian who is charged with safeguarding the property.
8 The name of the sales agent and the time, date and location of the sale.

Execution Reports must bear the signature of the Execution Officer and the debtor, if present; the custodian, and all those persons who have acted with reference to the report, in accordance with regulations.

Article 41 [Notice of Attachment]

The Execution Report must be published on the execution data publishing site within five days from the date of the seizure. This announcement is considered as constructive notice to all persons having an interest in the asset seized. The Execution Officer must serve the Debtor and all others with a right in the asset seized who have appeared in the proceedings before the Execution Judge whenever their addresses are known.

Article 42 [Custodian of Seized Property]

The Execution Judge shall order the custodian to safeguard the asset seized, but he must provide a guarantee or a co-guarantor who will guarantee that he will not act in a manner so as to harm the creditor. If the custodian refuses the custodianship, or fails to provide a co-guarantor or guarantee, the judge may appoint a licensed custodian.

Article 43 [Delivery of Seized Property]

In all cases the seized asset must be delivered to the custodian and signed for on the Execution Report. The custodian must not use the seized asset, lend it or subject it to damage. The Execution Judge can order the custodian to manage the asset if necessary and maintain any profits together with the original asset seized.

Article 44 [Custodian's Fees]

Where the Debtor does not remain in possession and a custodian is appointed, the wages of the custodian must be estimated and included in the Execution Order and charged as costs of execution.

Article 45 [Real Property]

Following the seizure of real property, the garnishee will be provided with a copy of the Execution Report. The property registry shall be provided with a copy of the Execution Order to be recorded in the property records.

Article 46 [Additional Remedies]

If the debtor fails to comply with an Execution Order within five days after service or in the absence of service, within five days of publication in a newspaper of general circulation, or fails to identify an asset of sufficient value to cover the outstanding debt; the

Execution Judge shall immediately order all of the following:

1. Prevent the debtor from traveling
2. Forbid him from issuing Powers of Attorney directly or indirectly, and all of its cases and its kinds.
3. Disclosure of the debtor's financial status and future income.
4. Disclosure of the debtor's commercial activity, including financial records and licenses.
5. A certified notice to him advising that adverse credit information including Notice of Default will be provided to credit reporting agencies.

In addition to the foregoing, the Execution Judge may issue the following orders in his discretion:

a. Prevent government agencies from dealing with the debtor, requiring them to notify the Execution Judge of sums owed the debtor and garnish any sums owed to the debtor.
b. Prevent financial institutions from dealing with the Debtor in any capacity.
c. An order to disclose information concerning the transfer of assets or cash owned by the debtor which may be issued to the debtor's spouse or children where the evidence suggests a transfer has been made. Where it is suspected that the debtor has attempted to secrete assets, a request for such an order shall be submitted to the Execution Judge.
d. Imprisonment of the debtor in accordance with the provisions of the law.

Article 47 [Investigation of Debtor]

The Execution Judge may question the Debtor, and impose sanctions on him, his staff or anyone who has dealings with him and who are suspected of aiding and abetting him in the transfer of assets in order to trace those assets. The Execution Judge may appoint an expert for the purpose of recovering any assets.

Article 48 [Return of Execution Order]

The original copy of the Execution Order and the data contained therein must be entered in the log of the court's Execution registry and its data filed.

Chapter Two: Auction of Seized Property

Article 49 [Auction Procedures]

Only qualified bidders may enter the auction hall. Qualification shall be determined in accordance with regulations established by the Ministry of Justice in cooperation with the Saudi Arabian Monetary Agency. Bidders must be proven solvent as determined by regulation and shall pay for any bids accepted and auction fees immediately after the auction.

Article 50 [Time and Place of Auction, Auction Procedures]

1. Auctions shall be announced at the site where the Execution Order issued for a date no sooner than fifteen days and no later than thirty days thereafter. A Notice of Auction shall be affixed to the door at the location of the seized asset indicating the day, time and place of the sale, the type of seized asset and its description. The Execution Judge may order the publication of the announcement in a newspaper of general circulation and the costs of publication shall be deducted from the proceeds of the auction.

2. The auction shall take place in the presence of the Execution Officer. The auctioneer will commence the auction by stating a minimum bid amount. The sale is not valid if the highest bid is less than the appraised value. If no bidders bid, the Execution Officer may set another day to continue the auction not to exceed two days in the future at which time the seized asset will be sold to the highest bidder unless the asset consists of real property,

precious metals or jewelry of any kind. The Judge may enter an order to stop the auction, and re-open the auction at a later date, at which property will be sold to the highest bidder.

The successful bidder must pay all fees immediately according to regulations.

3. If the successful bidder fails to pay the fees on schedule, there will be a new auction following the procedures as set forth in paragraphs (1) and (2) of this Article. The defaulting bidder is liable for any difference in the price of the property and any excess auction fees.

Article 51 [Conduct at Auctions]

Any manipulation of auction prices is prohibited, and the Execution Judge shall refer the matter to the Bureau of Investigation and Prosecution to conduct a necessary investigation if there is suspicion of collusion.

Article 52 [Redemption at Auction]

The Execution Judge shall halt the auction if the debtor pays the outstanding debt or if a portion of the sale of assets is sufficient to cover the existing debt and the costs of execution.

Article 53 [Auction Report]

1. The Execution Officer shall prepare a report documenting all steps taken and containing the name of the successful bidder and the sale price.

2. The Execution Judge shall award the asset to the successful bidder after money required has been deposited in the registry of the court along with a summary of the execution report and the Report of Execution, and the Order giving the bidder free and clear title. The sale order will be constitute an Execution Order.

Article 54 [Clear Title following Sale]

The Order awarding property to the successful bidder following an auction removes any lien or encumbrance on the asset.

Article 55 [Sale of Securities]

Sales of securities are subject to the financial markets system established by the Capital Markets Authority (CMA) and conducted by a person licensed by the Capital Market Authority (CMA) in securities sales. The Ministry of Justice and the Capital Markets Authority shall establish necessary controls for the sale of these securities, in order to achieve a fair price through performance guarantees.

Article 56 [Judicial Bank Accounts and Safety Deposit Boxes]

1. Bank accounts may be opened by the Court for the deposit and disposal of funds seized. Regulations shall specify the rules for the deposit of funds into such accounts.
2. Precious metals and jewelry shall be deposited in a safe deposit box maintained by a bank holding accounts of the Execution Court.

Regulations will be established to implement the procedures and provisions to facilitate the participation of banks with respect to the implementation of Execution Orders through the agreement of the Minister of Justice and the Governor of the Saudi Arabian Monetary Agency.

Chapter Three
Execution Proceeds Distribution

Article 57 [Necessity of Order]

The proceeds of an execution shall only be distributed by order of the Execution Judge to the creditors, and to all parties in the proceedings.

Article 58 [Settlement by Creditors]

If the execution proceeds are insufficient to meet the claims of the creditors, and they agree to an amicable settlement amongst themselves for distribution, the Execution Judge shall note their agreement in the record when signed by the judge and the Execution Officer. This record shall constitute a final judgment.

Article 59 [Distribution where No Agreement]

If the proceeds of the execution are insufficient to meet the claims of the creditors and the creditors cannot amicably agree on the distribution of the remaining proceeds, the Execution Judge shall note the lack of agreement in the record to be signed by himself, the Execution Officer and the creditors. The Execution Judge shall then issue an order providing for the distribution of the proceeds amongst the creditors, in accordance with the Shari'ah and legal principles.

Chapter Four
Execution on Debtor's Property

Article 60 [Funds held by Financial Institutions]

1. As specified in the regulations and in accordance with the rules of the supervising authority, garnishment of monies owed in the possession of financial institutions shall be subject to the following guidelines:

   a. Freezing the current account of the debtor, by that financial institution to prevent the account holder from withdrawing funds from his account. The freeze shall extend to subsequent deposits to his account. Upon approval of the Execution Judge, debts owed to the financial institution arising before the attachment may be disbursed from the debtor's account.

   b. Freezing investment accounts, by that financial institution to prevent the account holder from withdrawing funds from his account. The freeze shall extend to subsequent deposits to his account. Any cash balance shall be dedicated to meet debts owed the creditor and satisfying positions taken as of the date of garnishment. If the credit cash balance is dedicated to pay expenses due from stock exchanges or operations at the time of maturity or those created before notifying the financial institution of the attachment, these shall be subject to attachment procedures only after the close of trading hours.

c. The garnishee shall hold funds frozen in order to insure that the Debtor cannot withdraw these funds except upon approval of the Execution Judge taking into account the nature of the instrument, its maturity date and the consequences of early sale.

d. In the case of the attachment of safety deposit boxes, the execution officer will witness the opening of the boxes at the financial institution where their contents shall be inventoried and such inventory attested to by the execution officer, the staff of the financial institution and the debtor, if present. Keys to the safety deposit boxes shall be deposited into the registry of the Execution Court.

e. Attachment on the proceeds of policies of insurance by entering the attachment on the insurance contract record. Any compensation due the debtor shall be paid into the registry of the Execution Court.

2. Return of the attachment order shall be made to the Execution Judge within three days of service on the financial institution.

3. The Execution Judge shall order the financial institution to deposit with the registry of the Execution Court all sums due the debtor in accordance with paragraph (1) of this Article in the amount specified by the order of attachment.

Article 61 [Attachment of Securities]

1. Shares owned in companies not listed on the stock exchange shall be garnished at the Ministry of Commerce and Industry by noting the attachment on the record evidencing ownership of the company and entering the execution document in the commercial registry.
2. Securities shall be garnished through the Capital Markets Authority and return shall be made within three working days from service of the garnishment order in accordance with the following:
   a. Securities shall be garnished by restricting the debtor from transferring them, and
   b. The Exchange shall be ordered to withhold funds owed to the debtor with respect to the transfer of securities.

Article 62 [Attachment of Negotiable Instruments]

Negotiable instruments may be attached in accordance with the following:

1. If the check is in the hands of the creditor, the Execution Officer shall prepare the order of attachment and the amount of the check or a part thereof shall be collected and deposited in the registry of the court.
2. The amount of an endorsed instrument shall be garnished after notifying the holder of the execution order by the drawee bank when the payee attempts to cash the instrument. The amount of the check should thereafter be transferred to the registry of the court.
3. If there are no funds available to cover an instrument issued by the debtor, the Execution Judge shall authorize the holder to recover the amount of the check from the drawee bank or an endorser by depositing the instrument in the registry of the court. In case the drawer or endorser objects to payment, he may file a lawsuit within ten days from the date of the payment order and he shall notify the Execution Judge of the commencement of such suit and its contents. If the ten day period expires without the submission of a claim, the amount of the instrument shall be deposited in the registry of the court.

4. Bills of exchange and promissory notes held by the debtor shall be attached by depositing them in the registry of the court. If these instruments are not mature, collection shall be deferred until the time of maturity.

5. If the holder or endorser of the promissory note objects to the right of the creditor, he must commence an action in accordance with the provisions of paragraph 3 of this Article.

Article 63 [Instruments in Favor of Debtor]

Garnishment of bonds, promissory notes or instruments paying funds to the debtor in the future may be permitted by the Execution Judge taking into consideration the maturity of such instruments. The Execution Judge, the obligor and the debtor shall make an accounting of all amounts payable and the date of their maturity. If garnishment is approved, such instruments will be deposited into the registry of the court according to controls established by this law for each type of asset.

Article 64 [Intellectual Property]

Execution on intellectual property shall be effected by service upon the competent authority for the registration of intellectual property, by signing on the log of the content of the Order of Execution. The Execution Judge will be notified of the result of the garnishment within three days from the registrar's receipt of the Order of Execution.

Article 65 [Self-help by Creditor]

The creditor may use self-help to initiate a garnishment by service of a Notice on the debtor containing the information which must be contained in the Order of Execution. The garnishment is to be followed by an order from the Execution Judge or competent judicial authority within the ten days to confirm the right and validity of the garnishment. Failure to obtain an order within the prescribed time dissolves the garnishment.

Article 66 [Multiple Branches]

If the garnishee has more than one branch, service upon a branch is considered as sufficient with respect to the garnishee.

Article 67 [Failure to Honor Order]

If the garnishee fails to honor the order of the Execution Judge and freeze funds in its possession, the Executive Judge must, upon the request of the Creditor, levy on the property of the garnishee funds equal to the amount of the debt.

Section IV

Chapter One
Direct Execution

Article 68 [Use of Force Authorized]

If Execution has been ordered and the debtor has failed to honor the Order for at least five days, the Execution Judge may order the implementation of necessary measures including the use of force(police).

Article 69 [Fines]

If after the use of force the Execution remains unsatisfied, the Execution Judge may impose a fine not to exceed ten thousand riyals per day to be deposited in the registry of the court for each day in which the Debtor refused to honor the Order of Execution. The Execution Judge may, in his discretion, cancel part or all of the fine if the Debtor begins to honor the Order of Execution.

Article 70 [Injunctive Relief]

If forcible execution fails, and a fine imposed on the Debtor did not cause him to honor the Order of Execution during the period allowed for compliance by the Execution Judge, the judge may issue an injunction forcing the Debtor to comply on pain of imprisonment.

Article 71 [Effect on Agents and Employees]

The provisions of the direct execution are imposed on the legal representative of a private individual, or the employees of a Debtor who is obstructing implementation of the Order of Execution.

Article 72 [Eviction, Auction of Movable Property]

Eviction from real property shall be accomplished by the police by visiting the location of the property within five days from the date of service of the Order of Execution. The police may take possession of the property and deliver possession to the creditor, and may use coercive force to enter the property where necessary.

If the custodian of the movable property failed to be present, attend, or deliver movable property, the movable property shall be placed in the safe in the court registry. The Execution Judge shall order their sale at auction after two months unless the custodian redeems them, in which case an amount equivalent to their value will be deposited to the registry of the court.

If the executor is a creditor of the custodian, the procedures of this law shall be applied to the property of the debtor custodian.

Chapter Two
Execution in Matters of Personal Status

Article 73 [Applicability, Periodic Payments]
Decisions and judgments in matters of personal status are executed in accordance with this law where necessary to sell property to satisfy debts owing to a Creditor. If the implementation includes periodic payments the Order of Execution may so specify in accordance with arrangements as provided for by regulations.

Article 74 [Child Custody and Other Domestic Matters]
Judgments issued with respect to child custody and protection, the separation of the spouses are matters which relate to personal status and may be executed forcibly, even if that leads to the use of force (police) and entering homes to implement court orders whenever necessary.

Article 75 [Return of Wife to Marital Home]
Implementation of an order requiring the return of the wife to the marital home may not be executed.

Article 76 [Visitation with Minor Children]
The Execution Judge shall determine how to implement a judgment permitting visitation with minor children unless a previous judgment already so provides. Implementation is accomplished by delivering the child to an appropriate place other than a police station or similar place.

Section V
Chapter One
Insolvency

Article 77 [Debtor's Claim of Insolvency]

If a debtor fails to pay a debt by claiming insolvency, the Execution judge shall consider the claim only after completing those procedures requiring the disclosure of funds, interrogation of the Debtor and tracing assets in accordance with the provisions of this law. The judgment of insolvency shall include the reasons for the request, and shall be published in one or more newspapers of general circulation in the home of the debtor.

Article 78 [Insolvency and Concealing Property]

1. If a Debtor claims insolvency and it later appears that he has hidden his money, the Execution Judge may, taking into account the amount of the debt, impose a sentence of imprisonment not to exceed five years. Such judgment is subject to scrutiny of the Court of Appeal.
2. The Execution Judge shall summon the Debtor and question him on the state of his financial affairs on a regular basis not exceeding three months as determined by regulation.
3. The Implementing Regulations shall determine debts recoverable in insolvency according to the classes of debts and debtors, in coordination with the Ministry of Interior and the Ministry of Finance.

Article 79 [Debts due to Torts]

If a debt arises from negligence and the debtor claims insolvency, the judge shall interrogate the Debtor under oath in order to make a determination.

Article 80 [Bad Faith Insolvency]

If the debtor claims insolvency fraudulently or insolvency proceedings are commenced in bad faith, or if the Debtor fails to appear without cause and it is so determined by the judge, the judge shall complete the execution procedures, and shall refer the accused to the Bureau of Investigation and Prosecution within a period not exceeding seven days. Interested parties may petition the Bureau to initiate prosecution. If a prosecution is filed, the Execution Judge shall consider the case. In case of conviction, those penalties set forth in this law shall apply.

Article 81 [Notification]

1. The Execution Judge shall issue his order to those responsible for the assets covered by this law including money to be received in the future by the insolvent Debtor.
2. The judge shall notify the licensed person to record the insolvency in the Debtor's credit file.
3. The Creditor may seek enforcement in the future is the Debtor's financial situation changes.

Article 82 [Insolvent Establishments]

A company is subject to the bankruptcy rules as prescribed by law.

Chapter Two
Incarceration

Article 83 [Contempt]

Based on the provisions of this law, the Execution Judge shall sentence the Debtor prison the debtor if it is shown, after an examination of the evidence, that the Debtor refuses to honor an Order of

Execution. Imprisonment shall continue until the Order of Execution is obeyed.

Article 84 [Limitations on Incarceration]
A debtor should not be incarcerated in the following cases:

1. If it appears that he has assets sufficient to meet the claim which can be garnished or levied upon.
2. If he provides a bank guarantee, or a surety which is accepted by the creditor.
3. If he proves his insolvency in accordance with the provisions of this law.
4. If they are assets of the creditor unless the debt is in the nature of support.
5. If a physician certifies that the Debtor is suffering from an illness which cannot be treated in jail.
6. If the Debtor is a pregnant woman or she has a child not more than two years old.

Article 85 [Effect on Debt]
Incarceration of the Debtor does not extinguish the debt owed. Debtors so incarcerated shall be segregated from prisoners in criminal cases. Prison administrators shall permit the Debtor to take such action as will cover or settle his debt.

Article 86 [Agents and Employees]
Prison sentences shall be imposed upon the duly authorized representative of the person where the representative has obstructed the Order of Execution or authorized persons providing implementing services.

Chapter Three
Sanctions

Article 87 [Jurisdiction]

Criminal courts have jurisdiction to impose penalties provided for under this law. Matters may be referred by the Execution Judge to the Bureau of Investigation and Prosecution or upon an official affidavit from the aggrieved person.

Article 88 [Punishable Offenses]

1. A debtor may be punished with imprisonment for a term not to exceed seven years if he has committed any of the following offenses:
   a. Failed to implement the final judgment issued against him; is guilty of hiding or secreting his assets or failing to disclose his assets.
   b. Intentionally obstructing the execution by filing a lawsuit intended to obstruct the execution.
   c. Resisting the execution by threats or abuse by himself or through others on those appointed to implement the execution or against the Claimant or any other wrongful act done in order to resist the execution.
   d. Lying in his statements before the court, otherwise lying in the proceedings or providing incorrect information. In these cases the penalties stipulated for forgery shall apply.
2. All those who aid and abet the debtor in conduct punishable by paragraph (1) of this article shall be subject to the same penalty.

Article 89 [Government Employees]

A public employee may be punished by imprisonment for a period not to exceed seven years if he has obstructed an order of execution. This shall be considered as a crime of dishonesty.

Article 90 [Fraud]

A debtor who has incurred debt based on fraudulent behavior or who has squandered his money may be punished by imprisonment for a term not to exceed fifteen years and is subject to this penalty if shown that he became insolvent for this reason.

Article 91 [Other Penalties]

A person may be punished by imprisonment for a period not to exceed three years in each of the following cases:

1. Improper disclosure of a Debtor's assets by a person with access to official records. Anyone receiving such information shall be penalized in the same way as those who access such information without a court order unless a court order has permitted disclosure to such person.
2. Negligence or failure to carry out his duties by a bailee or receiver or neglecting or infringing or evading delivery or receipt of funds.
3. Deliberately influencing the price or providing false information concerning the fairness of prices whether at auction or otherwise by an Estimator, sales agent or participant at an auction.

Article 92 [Domestic Relations Penalties]

Anyone who obstructs the implementation of an order of child visitation, custody or guardianship whether or not a parent by imprisonment for a term not to exceed three months.

General Provisions:

Article 93 [Ministry of Justice]

The Ministry of Justice is the competent agency for dealing with administrative and financial affairs and shall assume the following responsibilities:

1. Licensing implementation services providers, such as:

a. Process servers.

b. Judicial sales agents.

c. Judicial receiver.

d. Judicial bailees.

e. Specialized companies to oversee the delivery process of movable assets to the Creditor.

f. Private sector providers of execution services upon the approval of the Council of Ministers to open this sector to private companies.

The regulations shall specify the license requirements, and also determine qualifying rules including the required bond, rules of conduct, their regulation, and the determination of standards for their fees and penalties that may be imposed on them for non-compliance.

2. Using one or more companies to implement Orders of Execution under the supervision of the judicial system.

3. Preparation of training materials to train the workers who will provide implementation services.

4. Publishing statistics related to implementation of Orders of Execution.

5. Exchanging information concerning Debtor assets with other countries.

Article 94 [International Treaties]

The application of this law shall not affect the treaties and other agreements with other countries and international bodies and organizations signed by the Kingdom.

Article 95 [Cause of Action for Delay]

Any person who is affected by the delay in implementing execution measures has a cause of action against the offending person before the Execution Judge to compensate him from any damage caused.

Article 96 [Effect on other Laws]

This law abolishes Articles 196 to 232 of the Shari'a Court Procedures Law, Royal Decree No. M/21 dated 1421/5/20 H and part z of Article 13 of the Law of the Board of Grievances, Royal Decree No. M/78 dated 19/9/1428H. This regulation shall supersede any other regulation inconsistent with its provisions.

Article 97 [Implementing Regulations]

The Minister shall issue executive regulations within one hundred and eighty days from the date of publication of this law.

Article 98 [Effective Date]

This law shall be published in the Official Gazette and shall come into force one hundred and eighty days from the date of publication.

ADDITIONAL REAL ESTATE LAWS

I.1 Measures for Selling Housing, Commercial, Office, Service and Industrial Units on the Map

MEASURES FOR SELLING HOUSING, COMMERCIAL, OFFICE, SERVICE AND INDUSTRIAL UNITS ON THE MAP*

* These measures have been issued by the Ministry of Justice circular No. 13/T/3600, dated 28.3.1430 AH, pursuant to the Council of Ministers resolution No. 73 dated 12.3.1430 AH.

I. It is prohibited to exercise the activity of selling any real estate units on the map for whatever purpose they may be used: housing, commercial, office, service, industrial, touristic or otherwise, to advertise the same in national or international media, to market the same inside the Kingdom or to display in fairs unless the approval of the committee under (2) hereof is first obtained.

II. A committee within the Ministry of Commerce and Industry comprising members from the Ministry of Municipal and Rural Affairs, Saudi Arabian Monetary Agency and General Housing Commission shall be formed with the task of conducting the following:

   a. Considering applications for exercising real estate development activities provided that the licence is issued within a maximum period of ten days from the date of the submission of a complete application;

b. Laying down technical and financial conditions for real estate developers;

c. Laying down conditions and specifications for expending from the security account for the project and supervising it, determining the responsibilities of the engineering office supervising the project, the chartered accountant and the inspection companies and calculating specialist quantities and determining their role in payments related to the expenses of the project;

d. Laying down the conditions related to the rights of consumers and the conditions of the operation of common utilities of the real estate development project;

e. Preparing a record that includes the arrangements and documentation related to the sale of units on the map in any real estate project;

f. Laying down the conditions related to reporting sold real estate and the mechanism of protecting consumers against selling a single real estate to more than one buyer by developers or brokers; and

g. Determining the documents necessary for registration in the real estate developers' record including the following:

1. The commercial register for individual establishments or companies,

2. Chamber of Commerce membership certificate,

3. Credit record integrity certificate from a licensed credit services,

4. Ownership deed of the piece of land to be developed,

5. Copy of the contract concluded between the main developer and sub-developer, if any,

6. Architectural designs and engineering plans approved by the appropriate authorities,

7. Form of sale contract between the developer and the buyer and dates of handover specified in days, and

       8. Copy of the contract concluded between the developer and the real estate marketer, if any.

III. A separate account shall be opened for each project after obtaining the approval of the above referenced committee to be named "The Security Account" with a bank licensed to operate inside the Kingdom. The said account shall be special for depositing the payments made by buyers of units on the map or the financiers of these projects. An agreement concluded for this purpose shall determine the conditions of managing the said account and the rights and obligations of contracting parties as decided by the committee in this respect.

IV. The Ministry of Commerce and Industry shall undertake the following:

    1. Providing a number of staff to act as secretaries of the committee; and

    2. Opening a record within the Ministry to be named "Real Estate Developers Record" wherein the names of qualified real estate developers are entered after obtaining the committee's approval of entering them in the said record and issuing certificates to this effect;

V. Any one who has been exercising the sale of real estate units on the map in the Kingdom before the issuing of these measures shall apply to the committee to adjust his condition as complying with these measures. The committee should consider each case separately in a manner that does not cause harm to the rights of buyers and the real estate developer within a period of sixty days from the date of issuing these measures. Extension for a further period may be given if there are certain objective reasons after obtaining the approval of the Minister of Commerce and Industry.

VI.

    a. In case the real estate developer violates the present measures, the committee shall issue a decision suspending his activity on a temporary basis taking into consideration the rights of buyers, provide the credit services company with information on the violation and submit to the Minister of Commerce and Industry about the actions to be taken against him as provided for in the regulations and instructions.

b. In case any fraud, covering up or procrastination to fulfil the rights of buyers is found in the real estate activity, the committee shall refer violators to the Investigation and General Prosecutor Commission, which, in turn, shall refer indicted violators to the Criminal Court to apply necessary penalties against him.

VII.

1. These measures shall be published in the official gazette and shall come into effect from the date of publication. The committee shall coordinate with the real estate committees at the Saudi Chamber of Commerce and Industry to advertise these measures through various means of information.

2. These measures shall remain effective until the issuing and coming into effect of the real estate development security account law.

I.2   General Housing Commission Act*

* Issued by the Resolution of the Council of Ministers No. 275 dated 28.8.1428 AH and Ministry of Justice circular No. 13/T/3232 dated 8.10.1428 AH.

Article 1

The following words and expressions, wherever they occur in this act, shall have the meanings given opposite to them unless the context requires otherwise:

Commission: General Housing Commission
Act: Commission's Act.

Board: Commission's Board of Directors.
Chairman: Chairman of the Board.
Member: Member of the Board of Directors. Governor: Governor
of the Commission.

Article 2
The Commission has a general corporate personality and financial
and administrative independence. Its head office shall be in the city
of Riyadh and has the right to establish branches inside and outside
the Kingdom.

Article 3
The Commission aims at providing suitable housing in accordance with the options catering for the needs of citizens and in accordance with programmes laid down by the commission, especially
to:

1. Facilitate the citizen's acquisition of a easily paid for house that
   meets the standards of quality within the scope of his income
   at the suitable time of his life;
2. Increase the percentage of ownership of houses;
3. Encourage involvement of the private sector in supporting
   various housing activities and programmes; and
4. Raise the percentage of offered houses of different types.

Article 4
To attain the objectives of the commission, the commission undertakes the following duties:

1. Prepare, update, develop and submit for approval comprehensive housing strategies for the kingdom as per the applicable
   official procedures.
2. Propose the laws, rules, policies and regulations related to
   the housing activity and propose amendments thereto as commensurate with the national strategies approved in this respect.

These policies and regulations cover, real estate mortgage, rights of lessees, owners of housing units, popular housing, general housing and development of lands for the construction of housing projects on them.

3. Lay down various and sufficient programmes to provide a suitable housing for citizens of medium income and below in accordance with the relevant objective standards and considerations as determined by the commission.

4. Encourage the private sector to effectively and actively participate in realizing the housing objectives and strategies in the Kingdom.

5. Determine the categories of citizens who are entitled to popular and charity housing programmes.

6. Develop guiding models of houses suitable for all citizens with specifications and standards that cater for quality and cost and that meet the approved building code and lay down guidelines and forms of contracts that include the rights and obligations of all parties.

7. Encourage the establishment of cooperative housing societies, coordinate their activities and review their motions of regulations.

8. Build suitable houses for the needy who are unable to benefit from the governmental and private lending and financing programmes.

9. Encourage charity societies, individuals and companies to contribute in building charity housing units suitable for the needy and provide advice and help when needed.

10. Prepare housing related studies and researches.

11. Create a housing database.

12. Represent the Kingdom in various functions related to housing.

Article 5

The Commission alone has the right to dispose with the lands that the government allocates for it for popular housing projects.

Article 6

1. The Commission shall have a board of directors comprising the following:

   a. Minister of Economy and Planning, chairman,
   b. Minister of Finance (Chairman of the Real Estate Development Fund), member,
   c. Minister of Social Affairs, member,
   d. A Deputy Minister of Municipal and Rural Affairs (selected by the Minister), member,
   e. Governor, member, and
   f. Four members among specialists and experts in the field of the Commission's activities to be appointed upon a resolution by the Council of Ministers upon the nomination of the Chairman.

2. The period of post for the members under 1.d and 1.f hereof shall be three years renewable for one time.
3. The remuneration for attending the meetings of the Commission by the chairman and members shall be determined upon a resolution by the Council of Ministers.

Article 7

The Board of Directors is the authority that controls administration of the affairs of the Commission and takes all decisions necessary for realizing its purposes within the limits of this act. It shall specifically have the following rights:

Article 8

1. The meetings of the Board shall be held at the head office of the Commission. When necessary, such meetings may be held at any other place inside the Kingdom.

2. The Board shall hold its meetings at least four times annually upon an invitation from the Chairman and whenever necessary for its interests. The invitation to the meeting shall be accompanied by the agenda. The Chairman shall invite the Board to meet when at least four members request the same. For the meeting to be valid, the majority of members should be present including the Chairman or his assignee. The resolutions of the Board shall be issued by majority of votes but votes are equal, the chairman shall have a casting vote. The objecting member may register his objection and the reasons of objection in the Board's minutes of meeting.
3. The deliberations and decisions of the Board shall be entered in minutes signed by the Chairman and present members. The Commission shall immediately report these decisions to concerned agencies in due course.
4. No member may abstain from voting or authorize another member to vote on his behalf in case of his absence.
5. No member may divulge any secrets of the Commission which have come to his knowledge.
6. The Board may invite to its meetings any one that it deems necessary to use their information and expertise without having the right of voting.

Article 9
The Commission shall be presided over by a Governor on the excellent rank who shall act as the chief executive office of the Commission. His duties and powers shall be within the limits of this act. He shall have the following authorities:

Article 10
The Commission shall have an independent annual budget issued by a Royal Decree in accordance with the arrangements of issuing the general state budget.

Article 11

1. The financial resources of the Commission shall consist of the following sources:

   a. The funds allocated for it from the state budget,
   b. The financial compensations that the Commission receives for the services and activities it undertakes in accordance with the provisions of this act, and
   c. Donations, gifts, wills and subsidies offered for it.

2. The lands received by the Ministry of Social Affairs in various regions for the construction of popular housing on them as well as the lands allocated for grants shall pass to the Commission.

Article 12

The financial year of the Commission is the same as that of the state. As an exception, the first financial year of the Commission shall start as of the effective date of this act.

Article 13

Without prejudice to the right of the General Auditing Bureau to control the accounts of the Commission, the Board of Directors shall appoint one external auditor (or more) from among persons of natural or corporate capacity authorized to operate in the Kingdom and determine their remuneration. If the auditors are more than one, they are jointly responsible for their activities before the Commission. The auditor's report shall be submitted to the Board and a copy of it shall be forwarded to the General Auditing Bureau.

Article 14

This act shall be published in the official gazette and comes into effective ninety days after publication. It shall supersede all contradicting provisions.

I.3   Law of Real Estate Ownership and Investment by Non-Saudis

Article 1

(a) A non-Saudi investor with natural or corporate personality, licensed to practice any professional, vocational or economic activity may acquire the real estate necessary for practicing that activity. It shall include the real estate required for his residence and for the residence of his employees, following the approval of the body issuing the license. The said real estate may be rented subject the stipulation stated in Article Five of this Law.

(b) If the license referred to includes purchasing buildings or lands in order to erect buildings on them and invest them by means of selling or renting, the total cost of the project, land and construction, shall not be less than thirty million riyals. This amount may be amended by the Council of Ministers. It is also stipulated that such real estate be invested within five years from its acquirement (possession?).

Article 2
Non-Saudi natural persons legally residing in the kingdom shall be allowed to acquire real estate for their private residence, following permission from the Ministry of Interior.

Article 3
On the basis of reciprocity, foreign representatives approved in the Kingdom may acquire the official seat of office and the residence for its head and members of staff. International and regional agencies, within the scope of the agreements governing them, may acquire their official headquarters, subject to obtaining permission from the Minister of Foreign Affairs.

Article 4

Possession of real estate for private residence, in cases other than the above mentioned, may be allowed upon the approval of the President of the Council of Ministers.

Article 5

Other than by way of inheritance, a non-Saudi may not have the right to ownership, easement or benefit of real estate located within the boundaries of the cities of Mecca and Medina. Acquirement of right to ownership shall be excepted if accompanied by endowing the owned real estate, in accordance with Shari'ah rules, on a specific Saudi entity. It shall also be stipulated in the endowment document that the Supreme Council for Endowments has the right to supervise (oversee?) the endowed property. However, non-Saudi Muslims may rent real estates within the boundaries of the cities of Mecca and Medina for a period not exceeding two years, renewable for a similar period or periods.

Article 6

Notaries public or any other competent body may not notarize any action inconsistent with the provisions of this Law.

Article 7

Implementation of the provisions of this Law shall be without prejudice to the following:
(a) Rights to ownership granted for non-Saudis under previous laws. Provisions of this Law shall be effected after its coming into force, upon transfer of the real estate ownership.
(b) Privileges included in the rules regulating real estate ownership by citizens of GCC countries.
(c) Acquirement of right to ownership or any other original right *in rem* (corporeal right?) to real estate by way of inheritance.
(d) Laws, Council of Ministers' resolutions and Supreme Orders prohibiting ownership at certain sites

Article 8

(a) This law shall replace the Law of Real Estate Ownership by non-Saudis in the Kingdom of Saudi Arabia issued by Royal Decree No. (M/22) dated 12/7/1390H.

(b) This law shall be published in the Official Gazette and shall come into force after ninety days from the date of its publication.

I.4   Lease of Forest and Arable Lands and National Parks Act

Council of Ministers Resolution No 1/428 dated 19/2/1421

Article 1

The terms are defined, wherever they occur, as follows:

Ministry: The Ministry of Agriculture and Water Resources.

Minister: the minister of agriculture and water resources.

Site: A land leased for tourism and entertainment purposes including forestland, arable and national parks.

Project: A tourism and entertainment investment set up on a site. Investment: Utilization of capital in tourism and entertainment oriented projects.

Investor: The natural person who is entitled to invest in the field of tourism according to this act.

Contract Form: The unified contract form for lease of forestland, arable and national parks for tourism and entertainment purposes.

Evaluation Committee: A committee formed by the ministry of agriculture to estimate the total cost of installations set up by the first investor on a leased land.

National Park: A large sample of the natural environment - including fauna and flora - within a certain major geographical location with a unique set of characteristics, requirements and objectives.

Arable: Uninhabited and cultivatable land suitable for tourism and entertainment projects.

Forestland: A land upon which are trees, shrubs or forest grass with a density not less than 10% regardless of whether wild or man-grown.

Article 2 Determining of sites and prerequisites of sites to be leased

1. The ministry shall determine the locations of the sites to be leased and draw a detailed map for each.
2. Sites shall be under the jurisdiction of the ministry and not belonging private owners.
3. Forest area covered by trees shall not be less than 10% of the of the total site space. Free space might be utilized for the construction of facilities provided as much space as possible be designated for growing decorative plantation.
4. Projects set up in such areas shall be strictly tourism and entertainment oriented.
5. Sites of spaces more than 100,000 sq. m. shall be leased through public tenders while sites less than 100,000 sq. m. shall be leased directly by the concerned committee. In all cases, the ministry shall determine the lease rate per sq. m.
6. In case of adjacent sites, license should not be granted to identical or similar projects unless approved by the ministry.

Article 3 Rules to be considered upon leasing a site through public tenders

1. All authorized investors have the right to bid in public tenders and they shall have equal chances in all aspects of the tender.

2. The announcement of a tender shall be published once in the official gazette and four other newspapers.
3. The announcement of a tender shall include the closing date and the place where offers of bids, enclosed in sealed envelopes, can be submitted. The period from the announcement date and the processing date shall not be less than 120 days.

Article 4 Tender Criteria

1. A bidder shall submit a feasibility study including plans and designs for the proposed site. Designs should comply with Islamic teachings and Saudi traditions and the study should cite the required water supply and resources for the project.
2. A detailed work plan covering all stages as well as current and futuristic requirements.
3. Determining the time frame and target date of operation.
4. Documents proving investor to be capable of executing the project.
5. A bank bond equaling 5% of the total cost of the project to be released upon the commencement of the project.
6. Foreign investors whether natural or juristic should obtain a license from the concerned authorities prior to bidding.

Article 5 Procedures of Site Leasing

1. Successful bidders shall be notified by a registered letter the address cited in their bid offer in order to sign a contract and the receipt of site within 30 days from date of notification. In case of a delay, the investor shall be sent another 60-day notification. Should the bidder fail to respond within time, the ministry shall cancel awarding them the tender and consider the next bidder.
2. Sites of areas less than 100,000 square meters shall be leased upon a request of an investor and the approval of the fore mentioned technical committee.

3. The technical committee shall be formed of the following figures:

President:

- Deputy minister of agriculture and water resources/ Agriculture Affairs.

Members:

- A representative of the pastures and forests department.
- A representative of the national parks department.
- A representative of the land investment department.
- A representative of the water resources development department.
- A legal advisor.
- A secretary of the pastures and forests department.

The committee shall receive investment applications, review them and respond according to the provisions of this act. In case of several applications for the same site, the best application shall be accepted.

Article 6 Lease Conditions

1. Contract duration shall be fifteen years renewable by a mutual agreement of the two parties.
2. Contract shall be effective from the date of signing and the investor shall be responsible for the entire site.
3. The lessee shall not assign the lease contract or part of it to others without the consent of the ministry.
4. The ministry shall terminate the lease contract for public interest after stating reasons for such action.
5. If the ministry decides not to renew a lease contract, a three-month notice shall be served to the lessee by registered mail.
6. If a lessee does not intend to renew a lease contract, he shall serve a three- month notice to the ministry by registered mail.
7. If a lessee decides to renew the lease contract he shall notify the ministry one year prior to the contract expiry date and if

renewal is approved, the ministry might re-estimate the lease rate and amend other terms subject to the consent of the lessee. A new contract shall be formatted then.

8. The lessee shall not execute work or take on duties not cited in the contract or the plans and designs of the project without the written consent of the ministry.

9. If the investor fails to fulfill any of the obligations set out by this act and the lease contract, the ministry shall notify them by registered mail to rectify the situation within 2 weeks. If they fail to respond in time, the ministry shall serve him a final 15-day notice. Failure to respond to the final notice shall result in termination of contract and investor shall indemnify the ministry for damages thereto.

10. If the lessee does not rectify the situation within the period cited in the final notice, the contract shall be terminated by the competent authority and the lessee shall hand over the site immediately to the ministry.

11. Without prejudice to the ministry's right to take legal action against a lessee in case the latter refuses to hand over a site, the ministry shall have the right to reclaim the site by force through concerned authorities and claim retribution for damages thereto.

12. If either the ministry or lessee does not intend to renew the lease contract, the lessee shall be obligated to make necessary repairs to all the installations on site under the supervision of the ministry prior to handing them over. In case of forceful hand over, the ministry might compel the lessee by all proper means to make necessary repairs.

13. Upon the termination of a contract, the evaluation committee shall estimate the expenses incurred by the lessee through investment on a site to be refunded by the new lessee. The first lessee might appeal underestimation to the minister, whose decision in this respect shall be final.

Article 7 Prerequisites of Investment

1. A lessee must obtain necessary permits before commencing construction works.
2. A lessee must consider using paints and material harmonious to scheme of the ambient.
3. A lessee shall comply with the following:
   - Providing necessities such as water, electricity, phone service, healthcare facilities, sewerage, garbage disposal, routes leading to the site etc.
   - Providing Saudi security personnel to maintain security and order.
   - Posting a sign bearing the project's name, license number and the name of ministry.
   - Providing first-aid equipment as approved by the health authorities.
   - Implementation of safety and security precautions related to traffic and civil defense in all designs and constructions and obtaining written certifications from the concerned authorities.
   - Fees for entering site must be agreed upon with the ministry.
   - Providing a full staff of managers and technicians to operate and maintain the site who should be medically examined prior to appointment. The lessee must also give due consideration to Saudization programs.
   - A lessee must operate the project at full capacity immediately upon completion. Partial operation shall be accepted only if the project is being completed in phases.
   - A full-time Saudi manager shall be appointed and delegated all powers to manage the site.
   - The lessee must keep the site clean and provide cleaning and garbage disposal equipments and dispose of waste as instructed be the authorities.

- The investor undertakes obtaining residence permits (Iqamas) and operation licenses for his foreign workers on site and renewing them on time. He undertakes not to employ persons not under his sponsorship and not to allow workers under his sponsorship neither to be employed by others nor self-employed in professions other than those they were recruited for. The investor shall not allow his foreign employees to inter- city travel without bearing their Iqamas and travel permits bearing his stamp and endorsed by the passports department. In case of breaching these provisions, the project shall be halted until the investor rectifies the situation and in case of repeated breach, the project shall be permanently shutdown and license revoked and awarded to a different investor.

Article 8 Investor Obligation

1. A lessee may establish a nursery on site to be utilized for forestation and transplantation according to the terms and conditions set by the ministry for commercial nurseries.
2. A lessee must preserve the trees and plants on site as well as tend to the appearance of the site and attempt to improve it without harming its natural characteristics. He must also provide the necessary services in a manner that would not damage the natural environment of the site.
3. A lessee undertakes not to grow new species of any type on the site without the approval of the ministry, to avoid the spread of possible plant-diseases and pests. He also undertakes to report immediately to the concerned authorities upon the discovery of an epidemic disease.
4. A lessee shall grant the right of passage through the site if deemed necessary.
5. It is not allowed to set up damns or any other installations that might disrupt or harm the natural flow of water or cause soil to

be swept on the site or nearby sites.

6. Lessees of natural parks undertake to develop them without changing or harming their natural characteristics.

7. A lessee shall be liable to repair damages occurring on the site or nearby sites as a result of construction works. Otherwise, he shall be subject to the penalties stated in the relevant laws.

8. A lessee shall take full advantage of the natural components of a park in order to make it as attractive as possible.

9. A lessee shall maintain the integrity of the park through having a minimal number of structures required to operate the park efficiently.

10. A lessee shall provide public access to the park and facilities without changing or damaging the natural characteristics of it.

Article 9 General Rules

1. National parks shall be technically supervised by a Saudi specialists or agricultural engineers with sufficient knowledge and experience.

2. The ministry shall have the right to such activities as those related to the preservation and increasing of the fauna and flora in national parks and the lessee shall enable the ministry to carryout its work.

3. The ministry or representative shall supervise the execution of the project. In case of failure to complete the project within the fore set timeframe, the investor shall be given a 4-month extension. The minister may withdraw the project from the investor if he fails to complete it within the extension time.

4. If investor fails to complete the project during the aforesaid timeframe, the minister may award the project to a different investor, who shall pay to the first investor all incurred expenses according to the estimation of a committee to be formed for this purpose.

5. The concerned authorities within the ministry may make routine inspections leased sites to ensure compliance to the terms of lease contracts.

6. The provisions of this act shall apply to all matters not regulated by lease contract.

7. The minister may delegate some of the powers stated hereof and belonging to him.

8. The minister may cancel or amend the provisions of this act.

9. This act shall be effective from the date of issuance.

I.5   Law of Ownership and Partitioning of Real Estate Units

Issued by Ministerial Resolution No. 40 dated 9/2/1423AH

Article 1

The words and phrases herein used shall have the following meanings:

1. Land: means the piece of land allotted for construction of a building and the related facilities and services, in accordance with the engineering drawings that have been approved pursuant to the building license.

2. Real Estate Unit: means a house, floor, flat, basement, shop or any part of the approved construction that may be partitioned and in respect of which a separate title may be claimed.

3. Owner: means any person/persons who own a Real Estate Unit.

4. Maintenance and Repair: means the works necessary for maintaining the real estate or an interest therein, whether with respect to a separate unit or the co-owned facilities, such as the lift, staircase and garden.

5. Co-owned Sections: means the land on which the building has been constructed, gardens, setbacks, framework, roof, entrances, staircase and all other sections of the building that are intended for common use whether jointly or separately, such as parking areas, corridors, fountains and lifts, unless otherwise agreed.

Article 2

1. Each owner shall be entitled to build on his land one or more floors, as may be permitted by the relevant laws and regulations and may divide such building into separate units according to the approved designs and drawings. He shall also be entitled to deal with all or any of these units separately.
2. The units in each building shall be numbered in a chronological order in such a way that each unit in the building shall bear a separate number.
3. The boundaries and measurements of the land and the buildings thereon shall be compatible to the approved drawings.
4. The content of the deed of ownership shall be compatible to the description of the land and the description of each unit. If the description in the deed of ownership differs from that of the land or of the units, the competent authority shall cause the entries in the deed of ownership to be corrected pursuant to the applicable regulations; a deed of ownership may be issued in respect of each unit.
5.
    (a) If a building is jointly constructed by two or more persons, it shall be co- owned by all of them as an undivided whole pro rata to their shareholding in the capital and other expenses, unless the contract provides otherwise.
    (b) The contract shall specify the names of all shareholders and the shares contributed in kind and those contributed in cash, the description of the land, number, date and place of issue

of the deed of ownership and the rights and obligations of shareholders.

Article 3

Shareholders shall be entitled to divide their undivided shares in the co-owned building. Any shareholder may be entitled to one or more units. Should they fail to agree to any such division, the interested party may claim through courts of law.

Article 4

1. Unless otherwise agreed, the owners of real estate units in any building shall be co- owners of the joint sections.
2. The partitions and walls between two adjoining units in any building shall be jointly owned by the owners of these units, unless proved otherwise. Neither of them shall be entitled to use its share in any manner prejudicial to the interest of the others.
3. Unless otherwise agreed, sections of the building whose benefit is restricted to some of the owners shall be jointly owned by these owners.
4. Unless otherwise agreed, the share of each owner in any indivisible section of the building shall be an undivided interest in the land and in the building and shall form part of the real estate unit for the purposes of any disposition..
5. The share of each owner in the co-owned sections shall be equivalent to the value of the divided part of which he is the owner.

Article 5

1. An owner of one or more real estate units shall share in the maintenance costs of the co-owned sections to which references made in Article 4, and shall also share in its management and repair costs, each according to his shareholding in the building.

2. Subject to the prior consent of the owners association, any co-owner may, at its own expense, make improvements of the co-owned sections or any part thereof, provided that any such improvement shall not affect or prejudice the interest of the other co- owners.

3. An owner of any unit shall maintain and repair its shareholding of the building, even though not in use, in order to avoid any harm to the co-owners or to the co-owned sections.

4. No owner of any real estate unit shall be entitled to relinquish its shareholding in the co-owned sections of the building with a view to avoiding payment of its share in the cost of maintenance, repair or refurbishment thereof.

5. An owner of the lower floor shall carry out the normal maintenance works so that the upper floors may not be affected or demolished. An owner of the upper floor shall not carry out any works in its building if any such work affects the lower floor and shall carry out the necessary maintenance works in order to avoid any harm to the lower floor.

6. If it is necessary to effect certain works within any unit of the building with a view to preserving the safety of the co-owned building or to improve or maintain the co- owned sections, neither the owner of any such unit nor the owners association shall be entitled to object to the carrying out of such works, provided that any such unit shall be reinstated to its previous state at the expense of the interested person directly upon completion of the necessary maintenance.

Article 6

As herein provided for, any owner shall not be entitled to use its share of the building excessively to the detriment of the neighboring co-owner. A neighbor shall not be entitled to claim against a neighboring co-owner for the normal and unavoidable practices. However, if any such practice exceeds the reasonable limits, he may be entitled to claim the cessation of any such practice, regard being had to the discipline, custom, nature of the real estate, location of each unit vis-Ã -vis the other units and the intended purpose of each unit.

Article 7

The procedure for the transfer of ownership shall be effected before the authority concerned with the notarization of leases, partitioning and the issuance of the relevant deeds pursuant to the applicable rules, subject to the provisions hereof.

Article 8

1. If ownership of the building is to be confiscated for public interest, whether such confiscation is in whole or in part, or in respect of the co-owned sections, such as the garden or the setback, each co-owner shall be entitled to be compensated pro rata to its shareholding in the building.
2. If a divided section of the building is to be confiscated, the compensation shall be paid only to the owner of the confiscated section.

Article 9

1. In case of co-ownership of a real estate comprising more than ten units which are owned by more than five co-owners, these owners shall form an association to protect the interest of the real estate. Such an association may be formed if the number of the units amounts to ten or less or if the co-owners are five or less.
2. The association of the owners shall enjoy a distinct juristic entity with a distinct financial liability and shall be registered at the Ministry of Labor and Social Affairs.
3. The resources of the owners association shall consist of the following:

(a) contributions of co-owners;
(b) amounts to be collected from co-owners with a view to meeting the obligations of the association;
(c) loans;
(d) donations and gifts; and
(e) the proceeds of investment of the relevant sections.

Article 10

The owners association shall appoint a chairman from within its members who shall chair its meetings and pursue the implementation of its decisions. The chairman shall be appointed by majority vote as provided for in Article 12 hereof. His term of office shall be three years and may be renewed.

The owners association shall, with the consent of three-quarters of its members, lay down rules that may ensure the best use and management of the joint real estate.

Article 12

Should there be no rules for the management of the real estate, or in the absence of provisions regulating certain matters, the owners association shall be responsible for the management of the co-owned sections and its decisions in that regard shall be binding, provided that all interested parties shall be invited to its meetings by registered mail. Its decisions shall be passed by majority vote pro rata the respective shareholdings of its members.

Article 13

The owners association may, by the majority vote provided for in Article 12 hereof, authorize the carrying out of any works or installations that may add to the value of all or any part of the real estate. Such works shall be carried out at the expense of the interested party, subject to the conditions as may be laid down by the owners association including the payment of compensation or the performance of any other obligation for the interest of the co-owners.

Article 14

1. The owners association shall be managed by a managing director to be appointed by the majority vote provided for in Article 12 hereof and who shall be responsible for the implementation of its decisions. Where necessary, the managing director shall take whatever action as may be necessary for the preservation, safe-keeping and maintenance of the co-owned sections and, except as otherwise provided for in the rules laid down by the association, he may ask any interested party to carry out any such action.

2. The managing director shall represent the owners association before courts of law and the other competent authorities and may file claims against any of the co-owners.

Article 15

1. Remuneration of the managing director shall be determined by the resolution pursuant to which he is appointed.

2. The managing director may be dismissed pursuant to a resolution to be passed by majority vote of the co-owners, as provided for in Article 12 hereof.

Article 16

1. In case of any damage to the building by reason of fire or otherwise, and unless otherwise agreed, the co-owners shall be responsible for its renewal pursuant to a resolution to be passed by the owners association, by majority vote of the members as provided for in Article 12 hereof.

2. If the building is demolished, the owners association shall take whatever action as it may deem necessary. In the absence of consensus, the matter shall be referred to courts of law.

Article 17

The minister of municipal and rural affairs shall issue rules and any other decisions as may be deemed necessary for the implementation of these regulations.

Article 18

These regulations shall supersede any contrary provisions.

Article 19

This law shall be published in the Official Gazette and be implemented ninety days after it has been published.

I.6 The Law Regulating the Government Rental and Eviction of Real Estates

Council of Ministers Resolution No. 234 Dated 16/9/1427AH

Rental Conditions

Article 1

Government agencies shall not rent real estates except where it is extremely necessary. Such rental shall be restricted to the needs of the relevant Government agency.

Article 2

Except where otherwise provided for, housing of personnel shall not be considered as a necessity that permits the rental of real estates. If the rental is intended for housing the personnel who are entitled to such housing pursuant to the regulations, the amount paid by the relevant Government agency for such rental, or otherwise, shall not exceed the amount of housing allowance of the beneficiary at the time of the lease agreement or any renewal thereof.

Article 3

The premises subject to a lease agreement shall fulfill the following conditions:

(a) Title to the premises shall be vested in the landlord, pursuant to a Shari'atic deed of ownership. This condition shall not apply to premises located in provinces and districts where suitable premises owned by a Shari'atic deed of ownership could not be found.

(b) The proprietor of the premises should not be an employee of the relevant agency (the tenant).

Leasing Procedure

Article 4

A Government agency wishing to enter into a lease agreement shall cause an advertisement to be published, at least twicely, within a period of fifteen (15) days in two (2) of the daily papers. Furthermore, advertisement in districts shall be effected by affixing the advertisements showing the wish of the relevant Government agency to rent some premises. In all cases, the advertisement should specify the type, area and the specifications of the desired premises, the duration and the intended purpose of the lease agreement.

Article 5

A Government agency wishing to take premises on lease shall set up a committee comprising three (3) of its employees to consider the submitted bids and recommend the acceptance of the most appropriate bid, regard being had to fitness of purpose and the amount of rental. This committee shall ascertain the safety of the premises and may elect to seek the assistance of an expert whenever it is deemed necessary.

Article 6

If the rental of the premises recommended by the committee referred to in Article 5 hereof falls within the limits prescribed in Article 15 hereunder, the Minister or his duly authorized representative, or the president of the independent agency or his duly authorized representative, shall be entitled to approve such rental following completion of the formalities herein provided for and the signing of the lease agreement. Should the rental of the recommended premises exceed the prescribed limits, the relevant Government agency shall notify the Ministry of Finance (State Properties Division) to inspect the premises and approve the rental prior to entering into the lease agreement.

Duration of the Tenancy

Article 7

(a) The lease agreement shall be for a period not exceeding three (3) years, which period shall be automatically renewable unless one of the parties notifies the other of his wish not to renew one hundred eighty (180) days prior to expiry of the lease term or any renewal thereof. The lease agreement may provide for the right of the relevant Government agency to extend the lease term following the expiry of the first duration for a period not exceeding three (3) years without obtaining the approval of the landlord. In any such case, the lease agreement may provide for the increase of rent by not more than 5% of the original rent where the required extension is for one (1) year and by not more than 10% of the original rent where the extension is for more than one (1) year.

(b) The duration of lease agreements may continue up to twelve (12) years provided that the premises forming the subject matter of the lease were to be constructed in accordance with certain specifications that were agreed upon by the two parties, namely: the landlord and the tenant.

Termination of the Lease Agreement and Eviction of the Premises

Article 8

The relevant Government agency (tenant) shall notify the landlord of its wish not to renew or extend the lease agreement on expiry of its term, by registered mail at the landlord's address kept by the tenant, unless it could be presumed that the landlord had knowledge of the tenant's wish not to renew. However, the tenant shall be entitled to terminate the lease agreement and evict the premises prior to expiry of the lease term if such premises have become unsuitable for use by reason of construction defect, or where the place has become unsafe.

Article 9

The tenant shall not be liable for compensating the landlord upon eviction of the premises in respect of the losses resulting from construction defects or normal wear and tear or the cost of repair or the additional buildings or the cost of removing such buildings where such removal was requested from and approved by the landlord prior to signing the lease agreement. However, the tenant shall be liable for compensating the landlord in respect of the losses resulting from the abnormal (improper) use of the premises, such as:

(a) The removal of fixtures or fittings including, inter alia, windows, doors, the contents of kitchen and bathrooms or the cancellation or use of these facilities for some other purpose.
(b) The demolition of a wall on the occurrence of cracks or ditches in the floors of the building.
(c) The filling of wells or green areas.
(d) Failure or malfunctioning of the air conditioning units, or the occurrence of a decay or damage in the electricity, water or sewer networks.

Article 10

Upon eviction, the premises shall be handed over pursuant to minutes which describe the condition of the premises and any damage resulting from abnormal use. These minutes shall be signed by a representative of the tenant and by the landlord or his duly authorized representative. In case of any objection by the landlord or his duly authorized representative with respect to the gravity or quality of the damage certified by those minutes, the landlord shall make and sign a reservation to that effect.

Article 11

The landlord shall be notified to receive the premises upon eviction or on expiry of the lease agreement, pursuant to a registered mail to be sent to the address kept by the Government agency (tenant) specifying the time of handover within a period not less than fifteen (15) days from the date of such notice, unless it could be presumed that the landlord had knowledge of the time of handover. Should the landlord, or his duly authorized representative, fail to appear on the prescribed date, the representative of the tenant shall, jointly with a representative of the principality or the province or the district, sign the minutes referred to in Article 10 hereof and deliver the keys of the premises to the relevant principality, province or district. By so acting, the liability of the tenant shall be deemed to have come to an end and no rent shall be payable in respect of any period following that date; the tenant shall not be liable for any damage to the premises not specifically mentioned in the handover minutes.

Article 12

The relevant Government agency shall set up a Committee comprising three (3) of its employees for listing the damage referred to in Article 10 hereof, assessing the amount of compensation and preparing detailed minutes to that effect within a period not exceeding thirty (30) days from the date of eviction. If the assessed compensation is in an amount not exceeding twenty-five percent (25%) of the annual rental or the amount of SAR 100,000, whichever is less, the relevant Government agency (tenant) shall pay such compensation to the landlord after completion of the formalities provided for under Article 14 hereof. If the compensation is assessed in an amount exceeding this limit, a Committee shall be set up from the Ministry of Finance, the General Auditing Bureau and the tenant in order to assess the amount of compensation and prepare minutes to this effect. The said committee shall finalize its job within a period not exceeding one hundred twenty (120) days from the date of eviction of the premises, provided that in assessing the compensation the Committee shall take into account the period that has lapsed between the date of eviction and the date on which it has inspected the premises.

Article 13

If the landlord carries out any repair or variation or change in the building following eviction of the premises but before the two (2) committees referred to in Article 12 hereof have made a list of the damage and an assessment of the compensation, as the case may be, he shall have no right to claim compensation.

Article 14 The relevant Government agency shall notify the landlord of the amount of compensation by registered mail to his address kept by that agency within a period not exceeding fifteen (15) days from the date of assessment of the compensation. If the landlord accepts such compensation, the Minister, or his duly authorized representative, or the head of the independent agency, or his duly authorized representative, shall approve the payment of such compensation. If the landlord rejects the compensation as assessed and approved, he shall be entitled to file a claim before the Board of Grievances within sixty (60) days from the date on which he has been notified of such compensation.

General Provisions

Article 15

(a) If the rental of the premises is SAR 200,000 or less, the formalities relating to such rental shall be completed by the relevant Government agency.

(b) If the rental of such premises is in excess of SAR 200,000, the formalities of such rental shall be completed through a committee comprising representatives of the relevant Government agency and representatives of the Ministry of Finance who shall assess the value of the land, buildings and the contents thereof, if any; the rent shall be computed according to the following percentages:

   1. Twelve percent (12%) for schools, security checkpoints, hospitals and medical centers.
   2. Ten percent (10%) for other Government directories.
   3. If the landlord's offer is less than these amounts, such offer shall be adopted.

Any of the provisions of this article may be amended pursuant to a resolution of the Council of Ministers.

Article 16

The Board of Grievances shall have jurisdiction over all disputes that may arise pursuant to the application of this law.

Article 17

The General Auditing Bureau shall carry out periodic inspection of the premises that are on lease to the Government with a view to ensuring that they are tenantable, properly used and fit for the purpose.

Article 18

The Minister of Finance shall, jointly with the Minister of Education and the Minister of Health, issue the implementing rules of this law and the standard lease agreement within a period of one hundred eighty (180) days following the publication of this law.

Article 19

This law shall be published in the Official Gazette and shall be implemented one hundred eighty (180) days following the date of its publication, and shall supersede any contrary enactment.

I.7   The Law of Disposal of Municipal Real Estates

Umm Al Qura Gazette, Issue No. 2454 dated 1/12/1392H(1)
Issued by the royal decree No. 64 dated 15/11/1392H

Article (1)

Public properties of the municipalities shall not be disposable, nevertheless, it may be permitted, within the limits prescribed by laws and regulations, to benefit from such with or without charges in such a manner that not contradict the purposes for which such is allocated.

Article (2)
Municipalities, may, within the limits of this law and the regulations thereof, dispose in the pertinent private properties by:

1- Sale or trading.
2- Lease.
3- Authorizing to benefit from such with or without charges.

Article (3)
In the application of the previous provisions public properties shall intend to mean properties (funds) actually or legally allocated (devoted) for public interest, and all the properties (funds) other than such shall be deemed private properties, and public properties which lack the capacity of allocation for public interest actually or legally shall be deemed as private properties.

Article (4)
Disposal in municipal estates shall be made in accordance with a regulation to be issued by the Prime Minister based on a recommendation of the Minister of the Interior and the Minister of the Finance and National Economy.

Article (5)
Such disposition shall be made based on a decision of the municipal Council, the disposition of the private properties of the municipalities having no Council shall made based on the decision of the Minister of Interior.

Article (6)
The person to whom such estate is to be disposed of, may not be a minister or undersecretary and the same may not be an employee

of scale eight and above in the administrative authority to which the municipality is affiliated or the same may not be an employee of whatever scale in the municipality undertaking the disposition or a member in the municipal Council issuing disposition decision. Such person may not be a relative of the parents, sons, grandson, spouse brothers and sisters or a known agent thereof. The right of such person shall not be transferred to any of the above mentioned persons for the whole five years following the disposition save through inheritance or will (bequest).

I.8   The Law of Non-Saudis Proprietorship and Investment of Real Estate

Royal Decree No. 15 dated 17/4/1421H

Article 1

a- The non-Saudi investor, whether a natural or juristic person who is licensed to practice any economic, vocational or professional activity may acquire real property necessary for practicing such activity, including that property necessary for his residence and the residences of his employees after obtaining the consent of the authority which issued the license. Property referred to under this article may also be leased subject to the provisions of Article 5 of this Law.

b- If the aforementioned license includes the purchasing of buildings or property for development whether through sale or lease, the total cost of the project, including the cost of land and the cost of building, shall not be less than thirty million Saudi Riyals. The Council of Ministers may modify such amount. The property shall be developed within five years of its acquisition.

Article 2
Non-Saudi natural persons who legally reside in the Kingdom shall, upon authorization by the Ministry of Interior, be permitted to own property for their own residence.

Article 3
Foreign accredited embassies in the Kingdom may–on the basis of reciprocity–own their official headquarters, and place of residence of their chief of mission in accordance with the agreement governing the establishment of diplomatic ties, provided that an authorization from the Minister of foreign affairs be obtained.

Article 4
Acquisition of property for a private residence may, by the agreement of the Minister of the Interior, be permitted in cases other than those mentioned above.

Article 5
No any other Saudi person may, other than through inheritance, obtain the right of ownership, possession or usufruct on property located within the boundaries of Mecca and Al Medinah. Ownership based on inheritance under the Islamic shari'a shall be exempted from such provision provided that endowment council shall have the right to supervise the endowed estate. However, a non-Saudi Muslim may lease property within the boundaries of Mecca and Al Madina for a period not exceeding two years renewable for a similar period or periods.

Article 6
A notary public or any other competent authority shall not authenticate any deed contradicting the provisions of this law.

Article 7

The enforcement of the provisions of this law shall not prejudice the following:

a- Rights of ownership accruing to non-Saudi nationals by virtue of the previous law. The provisions of this law shall take effect prospectively with respect to such property.
b- Privileges included in the rules regulating the possession of real property by the citizens of the Arab Gulf Cooperative Council.
c- Acquiring the right of ownership or any other right in or on other property through inheritance.
d- Laws and the Decisions of the Council of Ministers and the High order prohibiting ownership in some locations.

Article 8

a- This law shall replace the Law of Foreign Ownership of Real Estate in the Kingdom of Saudi Arabia issued by the Royal decree No. 22 dated 12/7/1390H (13/9/1970).
b- This law shall be published in the Official Gazette and shall come into force ninety days after publication.

I.9 The Real Estate Dealers' Offices Regulation

Published in the Okaz Newspaper, issue No 13157, Wednesday 26/6/1423H (4/9/2002)

Article 1. Regular class offices
Conditions:

1- The office owner shall be of Saudi nationality.

2- Holder of a general secondary school certificate or its equivalent.

3- Has obtained a computer applications course.

4- Has obtained an MS Word or MS Excel course besides some basic real estate courses.

5- The office area shall not be less than 40m2.

6- A would- be office owner applicant age shall not be less than 20 years.

7- Upon obtaining the initial approval the following shall be provided:-

    a- A computer set per the attached specifications.

    b- A telephone line.

    c- Purchase the real estate software and attend the pertinent training course.

    d- Signing an affidavit to use the software along with specifying the real estates information entry in the software, provided that they shall not be less than 100 real estate units per annum.

8- An affidavit and acknowledgement confirming that he has not been adjudged to be in violation of the shari'a, or been convicted of an offense involving honesty, and that he is not currently employed in a public or private position.

9- Provide an employee, of the same abovementioned qualifications, to fill for him when absent.

Benefits:

- Access to the Chamber of Commerce website and obtain needed information.
- The capability of entering the information in the computer.
- Access to the other program participant real estate dealers offices information.
- Monthly reports on the city real estate activity.
- An email address via the Chamber of Commerce.
- The office shall have the right to mediate in selling or renting the real estate units and obtain pertinent concessions.

Article 2. The Medium Class Office
Conditions:

1- The office owner shall be of Saudi nationality.
2- Holder of a general secondary school certificate or its equivalent.
3- Has obtained a computer applications course.
4- Has obtained an MS Word or MS Excel course besides some basic real estate courses.
5- The office area shall not be less than 80m2.
6- A would- be office owner applicant age shall not be less than 25 years.
7- Has a 5- year experience, at least, in this profession.
8- Allocate an SR500000 capital and register it in the Commercial Register at the Ministry of Commerce.
9- Upon obtaining the initial approval the following shall be provided:
    a- A computer set per the attached specifications.
    b- A telephone line.
    c- Purchase the real estate software and attend the pertinent training course.
    d- Signing the affidavit of using the software.
10- Obtain an advanced English language course
11- Obtain at least five courses in real estates activities and development, three of which shall be basic real estates courses and the other two advanced.
12- An affidavit and acknowledgement confirming that he has not been adjudged to be in violation of the shari'a, or been convicted of an offense involving honesty, and that he is not currently employed in a public or private position.
13- Provide two employees, of the same abovementioned regular class qualifications, to fill for him when absent.

Benefits:

- Access to the Chamber of Commerce website and get needed information.

- The capability of entering the information in the computer.
- Access to the other program participant real estate dealers offices information.
- Monthly reports on the city real estate activity.
- Surf the Internet through the Chamber of Commerce network and see the real estate advertisements.
- An email address via the Chamber of Commerce.
- The office shall have the right to mediate in selling or renting the real estate units and obtain pertinent concessions.
- The office shall have the right to possess and manage the properties of others upon pertinent agreements, endorsed by the Chamber of Commerce to guarantee the office commissions.

Article 3. Premium Class
Conditions:

1- The office owner shall be of Saudi nationality.
2- Holder of a general secondary school certificate or its equivalent.
3- Allocate an SR1000000 capital and register it in the Commercial Register at the Ministry of Commerce.
4- Has obtained a computer applications course.
5- Has obtained an MS Word or MS Excel course besides some basic real estate courses.
6- The office area shall not be less than 120m2l.
7- His age shall not be less than 30 years.
8- Has a minimum of ten years experience.
9- Upon obtaining the initial approval the following shall be provided:-
    a- A computer set per the attached specifications.
    b- A telephone line.
    c- Purchase the real estate software and attend the pertinent training course.
    d- Signing the affidavit of using the software.
10- Obtain an advanced English language course.

11- Obtain at least 10 courses in real estates activities and development, four of which shall be basic and advanced real estates courses.

12- An affidavit and acknowledgement confirming that he has not been adjudged to be in violation of the shari'a, or been convicted of an offense involving honesty, and that he is not currently employed in a public or private position.

13- Provide four employees, two of the regular class and two of the medium class qualifications, to fill for him when absent.

Benefits:

- Access to the Chamber of Commerce website and get needed information.
- The capability of entering the information in the computer.
- Access to the other program participant real estate dealers offices information.
- Monthly reports on the city real estate activity.
- Surf the Internet through the Chamber of Commerce network and see the real estate advertisements.
- An email address via the Chamber of Commerce.
- Advertise the office name in the Chamber of Commerce Trade Directory on the internet showing the office premium class.
- The email electronic inquiry forms.
- Prepare the automatic electronic answers.
- The office shall have the right to mediate in selling or renting the real estate units and obtain pertinent concessions.
- The office shall have the right to possess and manage the properties of others upon pertinent agreements, endorsed by the Chamber of Commerce to guarantee the office commissions.
- The office shall have the right to enter real estates stocks deals upon a license from the Chamber of Commerce.

I.10 The Realty in Kind Registration Law

Royal Decree No. 6, dated 11/2/1423H

Definitions

Article 1

The following terms and expressions shall have the meanings assigned opposite each:

The realty register: A group of documents that state, the description of each realty location, shariite status, the rights to and the obligations on it and the successive alterations that arise on such.

The realty area: A group of estate units demarcated by main streets or fixed devious landmarks.

The map: A geometrical cadastral drawing based on a national coordinates system that indicates the location of the realty area and unit or units, their boundaries, landmarks, serial number, lengths and areas.

The basic typographic maps: representation of a specific area of the Earth surface including its various features pursuant to an accurate map scale which represents a constant ratio between the linear dimensions on the maps and the analogous real dimensions on the ground.

The first entry: Inscription of the realty units in the realty register for the first time in condition at the time, and the allotment of a sheet for each of such according to the provisions of this law.

Demarcation and record-writing processes: The assertion of the nature of the realty unit, and preparing a map for such by an engineer or a surveyor wherein shall be indicated, its number and its statements, the writing of a record wherein shall be mentioned whatever the proprietor gives of statements and the supporting documents the statements of whoever claims a right to such, and the statements of the neighbors and others if necessary, pursuant to the form prepared for this purpose, and all such shall be effected under the supervision of a magistrate of the competent court.

The subsequent entries: Inscription of the dispositions effected on the realty unit after the completion of the first entry in the realty register.

The competent court: The court within the jurisdiction area of which lies the realty.

The realty right: a direct power ratified by the law to a person or, or more, authorizing disposition of the realty and monopolizing its benefits.

The original realty right: The right independent in itself which is not based on any other right that is adduced to the use of the subject of right object, or its exploitation or disposition of such.

The consequential real realty right: A right that is decided to the realty as a security to a personal right.

The easement right: A realty right that restricts the utilization of realty for the interest of another realty owned by another person.

General Provisions

Article 2

A real estate register shall be established wherein shall be confirmed, according to the provisions of this law, the realty rights and the alterations that occur in them.

Article 3

The register shall have an absolute confirmation power, and may not be objected to its statements after the elapse of the specified periods for objection stipulated in this law, unless based on the breach of the purport of Shari'a principles, or on forgery of such.

Article 4

The following shall be deemed a realty unit in applying the provisions of this law:

1- Each plot of land, including whatever therein of construction, plants and otherwise, which are located in one realty area, and is owned by a person or more, without a part of such being separated from the rest of the parts by a partition of public or private property, and without a part of such having rights or being subject to obligations, that the other parts do not have or are not subject to.
2- The land plot allocated for public utility, pursuant to the controls specified by the executive regulation.
3- The mines and quarries.

Article 5

It shall be permissible by virtue of a decision of the Minister of Justice, after agreeing with the Minister of Municipal and Rural Affairs, to consider an area of the residential areas or other, as one realty unit in its entirety, and a common sheet shall be allocated for it, and such shall be in the cases where it is difficult to apply the controls of the realty unit to it. A special index shall be prepared for entering the transaction and the rights pertaining to such areas, and shall be arranged according to the persons names which shall be attached to the pertinent sheet.

Article 6

A realty register shall be allocated to each realty register area, wherein a sheet shall be allotted to each realty unit on which the rights and obligations shall be entered, and the executive regulation shall state the manner of preparing this register and determine its statements and its pertinent documents.

Article 7

An alphabetical personal index shall be attached to each realty register, and its statement shall be derived from the latter, wherein a sheet or more shall be allotted to each proprietor, stating the realty units he owns, with his statements and the documents pertaining to him.

Article 8

The realty rights shall be entered into the realty register if they have resulted or have been prescribed due to one of the reasons of acquiring the realty rights in the manner acknowledged by the Islamic Shari'a, and the executive regulation shall explain the conditions and the procedures of entering such rights.

Jurisdiction

Article 9

Each of the Ministry of Municipal and Rural Affairs and the Ministry of Justice, shall undertake the process of the realty registration and documentation according to the following:

1. The administration competent in lands and survey at the Ministry of Municipal and Rural Affairs shall undertake listing the realty units, undertake the cadastral works, prepare and update the necessary maps and execute the land information systems,

and the Minister of the Municipal and Rural Affairs shall issue the decisions and the instructions necessary for such.

2. The administration competent in the realty registration and documentation at the Ministry of Justice, shall undertake entering and documenting the rights pertaining to the realty units located within its area of jurisdiction, but if the realty unit is located within the jurisdiction area of multiple administrations, it shall be obligatory to make the entry at each of such, and the entry made at one of them shall have no impact save as to part that lies within the area of its jurisdiction.

Article 10

The originals of the instruments and the verdicts pursuant to which the entry is effected, and the registers and the documents relating to the entry shall be kept at the realty register administration, and shall not be transferred outside it. It shall not be permissible to other than the judicial authorities or whomsoever delegated by them of the experts and the consideration panels to review them and shall be excluded from such the documents pertaining to the entry of the military installations and the economic projects of national nature, and shall be kept at the seats of the governmental authorities to which they belong, and the provisions of secrecy prescribed in their special laws shall be observed.

Maps

Article 11

The entry of the realty units in the realty register shall be based on the following plans:

1- The original typographic maps.
2- The realty unit map.

3- The realty area map.

Article 12
Each realty unit shall have an independent map illustrating its location, boundaries, lengths, area and features and whatever of installations therein the constructions on it, and the numbers of the neighboring units.

Article 13
Each realty area shall have a cadastral map or maps, illustrating plans, the realty units located therein and their numbers. Their preparation shall be based on the original typographic maps and the maps of the realty units constituting such. they shall not be deemed final save after the completion of the demarcation and the record- writing processes.

Article 14
Copies of the realty units plans shall be based on request, be given to the concerned persons after the payment of the prescribed fees.

The Initial Title Document

Article 15
This law shall be gradually applied, and the Minister of Justice-after agreeing with the Minister of the Municipal and Rural Affairs, shall issue a decision specifying the realty area or areas in which the application of this law starts, and the decision shall be published in the Official Gazette, and made public in the methods specified by the executive regulation.

Article 16

The Magistrate who supervises the first entry shall, upon the publication of the Minister of Justice's decision indicated in Article (15), issue a decision specifying the date of the start of the processes of demarcation and record- writing, and such shall be published in the official gazette at least sixty days prior to the start of such processes, and it shall also be announced in the methods specified by the executive regulation, and the announcement shall include an invitations to the persons concerned, or whoever legally represent them, to give directions to the locations of their realties, state their rights and to produce supporting documents on the dates and the places specified for such.

Article 17

The land and survey administration shall supply the necessary maps for the demarcation and record- writing processes, and shall undertake listing the realty units and demarcate each realty unit with fixed marks owned by the state.

Article 18

Each authority shall produce whatever in its possession of statements and documents pertaining to the conduct of the entry to the realty registration Administrations, and document them within thirty days as of the date of their request.

Article 19

Whosoever takes possession of the realty unit, whatever the reason, shall be obligated enable the officials assigned with the cadastral processes, to conduct the operations of the demarcation and emplacing the marks, necessary for such.

Article 20

The number, the boundaries, the lengths, the area, the erected constructions, the name of the proprietor or the proprietors and their shares, the neighboring realty units, the statement of the rights and the obligations the realty is subject to, the date of its establishment, and its proprietors, shall be entered in on the sheet of the estate unit as explained by the executive regulation.

Article 21

In case of the ownership title- deeds contradiction, concerning one realty unit, the rights shall be entered in the name of the person whom it becomes evident to the Magistrate supervising the first entry that he is the owner of the right, and report of such shall be attached to the sheet of the realty unit.

Article 22

The processes of the first entry in the realty register shall be conducted under the supervisions of a Magistrate from the court which the realty lies within its jurisdiction area with the aid of a number of the engineers and the surveyors, whose assignment decision shall be issued by the Ministry of Municipal and Rural Affairs, and they shall be subordinate to it as to whatever pertains to the technical and administrative affairs.

Article 23

The Minister of Justice shall be entitled to postpone, for a maximum period of three years, the processes of demarcation and record-writing of any realty unit, based on a substantiated recommendation from the magistrate supervising the first entry, if he deems that public interest requires such.

Article 24

After the completion of the demarcation and record- writing processes, a pertinent record to be signed by the Magistrate who supervised the first entry, shall be prepared, the statements of the demarcated realty units shall be announced, and the announcement shall include an invitation to the concerned persons to review the detailed statements of their units, the date of objection to such, and, at the same time, a notification shall be sent to each of them wherein shall be mentioned whatever was confirmed in their names of realty units in the demarcation and record- writing tables and whatever they have of rights, and subject to of obligation.

The indicated announcement and notification shall be in the manner specified by the executive regulation.

Article 25

The persons concerned shall be entitled to object to the result of the processes of demarcation and record- writing within a period of sixty days as of the date of announcing their completion, and the entry shall be suspended until such objections are determined on.

Article 26

The Magistrate supervising the first entry shall issue a decision on forming a committee to consider the objections indicated in Article (25), comprising of a member assigned by the Magistrate and a technician nominated by the Ministry of Municipal and Rural Affairs. The committee shall carry out the required investigation and inspection, and prepare a report of such, to be referred to the Magistrate within thirty days as of the date of its receiving the objection. The Magistrate shall issue a decision on either confirming the existing status or rectifying it. And the concerned persons shall be informed of such decision.

Article 27

The demarcation and record- writing records to which no objections were submitted, shall be brought before the Magistrate supervising the first entry according to the serial numbers of the realty units. If he is ascertained of their authenticity, he shall attest them and order their entry in the realty register, otherwise, he shall order the completion of the shortage aspects and the conduct of the necessary investigations; and then he shall issue a decision on attestation or rejection, and in the latter case the decision shall be substantiated.

Article 28

Each interested person shall have the right of objection to the statements entered on the realty unit sheet, and to request from the Magistrate supervising the first entry to alter them, and such shall be within a year as of the date of their entry in the realty register and it shall be permissible by virtue of a decision from the Minister of Justice to extent such period one additional period or periods not exceeding one year. The procedures stated in the executive regulation shall be observed in considering, and determine on the objection.

Article 29

The Magistrate supervising the first entry shall prepare a serial statement of the realties to which objections were submitted, and such shall be considered according to the date of filing the case or submitting the application, and the Magistrate may seek the help of the Ministry of Municipal and Rural Affairs in preparing the statements' memorandum, and the pertinent remarks before considering the objection.

Article 30

The effect of the first entry pertaining to the realty units subject of objection, shall be suspended till the issuance of the verdict of the Magistrate supervising the first entry, or his decision concerning them, and the Magistrate shall expeditiously determine on the objection, even if the concerned persons do not attend, after making sure that they were being informed of the date of considering the objection, in the manner specified by the executive regulation.

Article 31

The cases and the applications submitted in objection to the first entry in the realty register, shall not be heard before any judicial authority, after the elapse of the periods indicated in Articles (28, 34) save pursuant to the provision of Article (3).

Article 32

The verdicts and the decisions issued by the Magistrate supervising the first entry concerning the applications and the cases filed in objection to the first entry, shall be announced, and the case parties and the applicants shall be notified of such, and these verdicts and decisions shall be final in the following two cases:

1- If the alteration required in the statements of the register are agreed upon by the all concerned persons whose names are stated on the sheets of the realty units.
2- If the required alteration does not affect the right of any of the persons whose names are stated in the realty register.

Article 33

With the exceptions of the cases stipulated in Article (32), the concerned persons may apply for the cassation of the verdicts issued by the Magistrate supervising the first entry within thirty days as of the date of their pronouncement.

Article 34

It shall be permissible to object against the statements entered in the realty register before the competent court, within two years as from the date of entry in the register, if new evidences or documents appear which have not been formerly available to produce.

Article 35

Whosoever was a minor or legally incapacitated at the time of the entry in the realty register, shall be entitled to object to such before the competent court within five years as from the date he reaches the legal age as to the minor or within two years of the date on which he restores his legal capacity as to the legally incapacitated person.

The Entries subsequent to the first Entry

Article 36

It shall be obligatory to enter in the realty register all the dispositions leading to the establishment of one of the in kind realty original or consequential rights, or the transfer, or alteration, or removal of such; and also the final verdicts confirming some of such. And shall be included in such dispositions the realty division, the legacy, the endowment, inheritance and pawning, and shall not take effect on the others save as from their entry date.

Article 37

It shall be obligatory to enter lease contracts, the deeds that concern the utilization of the estate for more than five years, the quitclaims and the orders of payment of advance rent of more than three years, and the final decisions confirming some of such, in the realty register, and the non- entry of such rights, shall make it render than in effective against others in whatever, in excess of the aforementioned periods.

Article 38

It shall be obligatory to enter the right confirmed by inheritance if it includes realty rights, and till the completion of such entry, it shall not be permissible to enter any disposition by the heir concerning any of such rights.

It is permissible to restrict entering this right to a part of the legacy realties, and in such case, it shall not be permissible to enter any disposition by the heir, save within the limits of his legitimate share.

Article 39

It shall be obligatory to countersign, in the realty register, the instruments in writing confirming any debt owed against the legator, and the creditor of the legacy shall inform the concerned persons of the existence of the debt prior the tick off, to countersignature; and such countersignature shall not be used as evidence save as from the date of its occurrence, Nevertheless, if the countersignature has been effected within a year as of the date of the entry indicated in Article (38), the creditor shall have the right to claim his right from whosoever received from the heir any real realty right, and entered it prior to such countersignature.

Article 40

Cases pertaining to a realty right or to any of the dispositions to, shall be countersigned in the realty register based on the request of the competent courts, after being entered therein; whenever such cases include an application for the alternation in the statements of the register, and the case shall not be heard, save after producing whatever confirms occurrence of countersigning the content of such cases.

Article 41

Countersigning the cases in the realty register shall entail that the plaintiff's right, if prescribed by a final verdict, shall be an evidence against whomsoever were entailed rights or statements in their favour were inscribed in the realty register after effecting the mentioned countersignature, and such shall be whenever the verdict is entered within fives years as from the date on which it became final, and the five years term shall, concerning the final verdicts issued prior to the effectiveness of this law, start as from the date of its enforcement in the realty area.

Article 42

It shall be obligatory to countersign announcing the desire adopt preemption on the sheets of the preempted realty units, and such shall entail that the right of the pre- emptor, if decided by a final verdict entered in the register, shall be an evidence against whomsoever entailed realty rights after effecting the countersignature, and such shall be whenever the verdict is entered within five years as from the date on which it became final. The five years period, shall, concerning the final verdicts issued before the enforcement of this law, start as from the date of its effectiveness on the realty area.

Procedures for Recording Subsequent Records

Article 43
The initial record shall be submitted, by the concerned persons or their legal representatives, to the realty registration and documentation administration which the realty unit is located within the area of its jurisdiction, and the title deed and the supporting documents shall be attached to the application, and the administration shall prepare a journal wherein shall be recorded the applications of the concerned persons according to the time and date of their submission in the manner by the executive regulation. It is impermissible to make the entry if the sheet of the realty unit includes entries precluding disposition of such.

Article 44
The entry application shall be considered null and void if the applicant does not submit the statements and the documents supporting the application, and necessary to effect it, within a year of its submission date, and this term shall be extended once for another year if he submits an application for extending such term fifteen days prior to the elapse of the first year.

Article 45
If more than one application are submitted to the realty registration and documentation administration concerning the same realty unit, they shall be examined according to the precedence of their

listing in the journal, and such shall be in the manner specified by the executive regulation.

Article 46

If it is impossible to complete the process of the first preceding application due to a shortage or fault in the statements or the documents, the concerned person shall be notified of such to rectify it within fifteen days as of the notification date ; if the applicant fails to do so, the director of the realty registration and documentation administration shall be entitled to issue a substantiated decision rejecting the application, or extinguishing and abolishing its precedence or suspending the procedures concerning the subsequent of such, applications, as the case may be, and the concerned persons shall be informed of such, and the procedures of the application subsequent to application which it was decided to reject or to extinguish its precedence shall be considered after the elapse of fifteen days as of the notification date.

Article 47

Whomsoever, notified of the rejection of his application, the extinguishment of his precedence or the suspension of the procedures, shall be entitled to complain to the director of the realty registration and documentation administration within fifteen days as from his notification date of such date. If the director of the administration accepts his complaint, he shall order the entry, whereas if he rejects it, he shall commit the complaint to the competent court to expeditiously determine on it, with a cassated verdict, and to suspend considering the subsequent applications until determination on such.

Article 48

Entering the instrument deeds in the realty register shall be according to their order indicated in the journal and the date of their entry in such journal.

Article 49

A pecuniary consideration, not less than one hundred riyals and not exceeding five thousand riyals, shall be collected for the entries subsequent to the first entry, and for producing alternative documents, certificates and maps, and the executive regulation shall specify the values of such consideration and the manner of their collection.

The Council of the Ministers shall be entitled to modify such consideration.

Alteration and Correction of the Realty Registry

Article 50

It shall not be permissible to conduct any alteration in the records of the realty register, save based on the application of whosoever entitled to disposition of the rights entered therein, or pursuant to final judicial verdicts in the manner specified by the executive regulation.

Article 51

The applications and their pertinent documents which may lead to alteration in the cadastral statements shall be referred to land and survey administration, to investigate them and return them to the realty registration and documentation administration, accompanied with the result of the investigation.

Article 52

The director of the realty registration and documentation administration shall, on his own accord, or based on the request of the concerned person, and prior to the entry, be entitled to rectify the purely material errors on the sheet of the register, but if the entry was effected, it shall not be permissible to conduct such rectification save after notifying the concerned persons in, as the manner specified by executive regulation, and the director of the administration shall write a record wherein he explains the error, its cause, how it was detected, and the pertinent action taken.

Article 53

The competent authority at the Municipality shall be obliged to inform notify the realty and documentation administration of the building and demolition licenses granted to the concerned persons concerning the realty unit listed in the realty register for countersigning such opposite each realty unit in the manner specified by the executive regulation.

Article 54

The proprietors of the realty units shall be obligated to inform the realty registration and documentation administration of any change arising in the realty unit due to construction, or addition, or alteration or removal of buildings, and such within ninety days as from the date of this alteration, and an attested certificate from the competent authority shall be attached, and the updating of the statements in the realty register shall be made based on such.

Article 55

The director of the realty registration and documentation administration shall be entitled to issue a decision an adding any licensed, existing on the ground alteration not confirmed in the realty register.

Article 56

Each person of interest shall have the right to request the court to urgently erase the countersignature indicated tick prescribed in Articles (39 and 40), and the court shall order the erasure of any debt instrument is not confirmed according to Shari'a, or whenever it becomes evident clear to the court that the case based on which the countersignature was effected, the tick was made, was not filed save for a malicious purpose.

Article 57

The realty registration and documentation administration shall be obligated to notify each person whose rights have been altered, or ceased to exist as a result of an entry, erasure, countersignatures or rectification; and shall also notify the land and survey administration of all the alterations which arise in all the statements of the realty register, and such shall be listed in details in the title deed and the certificates reproduced from the register, pursuant to whatever specified by the executive regulation.

Article 58

If the erasure is cancelled, the entry of the right shall regain its original category in the realty register; nevertheless, this cancellation shall have no retroactive effect on the entries which were made in the period between the erasure and the cancellation.

Article 59

The persons injured by the entry in the realty register shall be entitled to claim compensation from the causer and the beneficiary of such entry whatsoever confirmed as unrightfully effected.

The effect of division and merger on the realty units' rights and obligations.

Article 60

If the realty unit subject to easement is divided, the easement right shall remain entitled to each part of such, provided that it doesn't increase the burden falling on the servient realty, but if the easement does not, in fact, benefit save only one of such parts, the proprietor of the servient realty shall be entitled to request the competent court to remove such right from the other parts.

Article 61

If the servient realty is divided, the easement right shall remain effective on each part of it, but if that right is not, in fact, used or cannot be used in some of the parts, the proprietor of each part of such shall be entitled to request the competent court to remove the easement from his part.

Article 62

The realty registration and documentation administration shall notify the proprietors of the dominant realty units and the servant ones in the two cases stipulated in Articles (60 and 61); and in case of dispute amongst the concerned persons, the matter shall be committed to the competent court.

Article 63

The easement rights shall be terminated if the both the servant and the dominant properties are possessed by one proprietor, and the realty registration administration shall automatically delete such erase without the need of an application from the proprietor.

Article 64

If the realty unit which bears an in kind consequential right is divided into two or more realty units, each new realty unit shall bear the proper right, the new proprietors may agree with the proprietor of the sequential right to split it in such a manner that each new shall not bear save a part of it specified by the agreement.

Article 65

If two realty units, one bearing in kind sequential right and the other does not, merge together, the sequential right shall extend to include the whole new realty unit, regardless of the consent of the proprietor of the right, but if each of the two units bears an independent in kind right, it shall be obtain the proprietors of the rights consent to the merger.

Article 66

The multi- flat and multi- floor realty shall be deemed as one realty unit, and a sheet shall be allotted for it in the realty register, and complementary sheets bearing the names of the proprietors of the flats and the floors, shall be attached to it.

Title Deeds and Certificates

Article 67

Each proprietor shall be delivered a copy of the sheet of the realty unit that he owns, and shall be called "title deed" If the realty unit is in joint ownership, each proprietor shall be delivered a title deed bearing all the names of the joint owners.

Article 68

Based on their application, a certificate of the statements entered in the realty register, shall be delivered to the concerned person after paying the prescribed pecuniary consideration.

Article 69

It shall not be permissible to deliver another title deed save after confirmation of damage or loss of the first title deed, and the delivery shall be after the consent of the director of the realty registration and documentation administration and the payment of the prescribed pecuniary consideration.

Article 70

Based on their request, demand the concerned persons shall be delivered a certificate of compatibility of the title deed to what is confirmed in the realty register, after paying the prescribed pecuniary consideration.

Article 71

Regarding the cases indicated in Article (40) which are under consideration before the court at the time of the effectiveness of this law and which have not been countersigned, it shall not be permissible to continue considering them save after countersigning such in the realty register, and the plaintiffs of such cases shall be granted sixty days respite, as from the date of the start of the demarcation and record- writing processes in the estate area, and if they fail to produce a certificate of the occurrence of the countersignature in the first session after the elapse of the respite, it shall be obligatory not to hear the case.

Article 72

Concerning the realty dealings during the first entry procedures, following provisions shall be observed:

1- Dealings conducted on the realty units of which the demarcation and record- writing records have been prepared and no appeals regarding them were submitted, shall be presented to the Magistrate supervising the first entry to consider them according to Article (27), without being bound by the serial numbers of the realty units.

2- The impact of dealings conducted during consideration of the objections to the demarcation and record- writing records before the Magistrate supervising the first entry, shall be suspended until the determination on such objections.

3- Dealings conducted after the determination on the previously indicated objections shall be submitted to the realty registration and documentation administration in order to consider their entry pursuant to the provisions of this law.

Penalties

Article 73

Without prejudice to any severer penalty stipulated in another law, whosoever commits one of the following acts shall be punished with a fine not less than five thousand riyals and not exceeding one hundred thousand riyals:

a- Attaining, by evil intention, the entry of a realty in the name of other than its proprietor, or unrightfully entails an in kind right on such.

b- Filing a malicious case.

c- Attiring or destroying the marks of the demarcation of the realty units or destroys them, and shall be obligated to pay the expenses of restoring them to their previous positions.

d- Telling or testifying in favor of a non- existent in kind right, or refraining from telling about the existence of an in kind right he knows.

Article 74

Without prejudice to any severer penalty stipulated in another law, shall be punished with a fine not exceeding ten thousand riyal whosoever:

a- fails to conduct the notification stipulated in Article (54).

b- refrains from appearing before the magistrate supervising the first entry to conduct the procedures of the demarcation and record-writing, in despite being correctly served the note of such.

c- commits an act that may impede the demarcation and record-writing procedures.

d- refrains from submitting the documents indicative of ownership.

Article 75

Considering the violations to the provisions of this law, and whatever they deem of investigations shall be undertaken by committees formed by a decision from the Minister of Justice, at the places, wherein he deems that the need requires the formation of committees. Each committee shall be comprised of a representative of each of the Ministry of Justice, the Ministry of Municipal and Rural Affairs and the Ministry of Interior, and any person against whom a punishment decision was issued, may complain against it before the Grievances Board within sixty days as from the date of his notification of the decision.

Article 76

The effective laws of the realty registration shall be applied to the realties not included in this law, until the issuance of what implies their inclusion in this law pursuant to Article (15).

Article 77

The Minister of Justice shall, in agreement with the Minister of Municipal and Rural Affairs, issue the executive regulation of this law, which shall be published in the official gazette, and shall be effective as from the date of the enforcement of this law.

Article 78

This law shall be published in the official gazette, shall be effective after a year as from its publication date and shall cancel all contradictory provisions.

I.11   Law of Time-Share Properties

Royal Decree No. M/52 dated 20/8/1427H (October 2006

Article 1 Definitions

The following words and phrases, wherever mentioned in this Law, shall have the meanings expressed next to them, unless the context requires otherwise:

Holiday Properties: Hotels, furnished apartments, resorts and other units meant for tourist accommodation, including holiday properties in Mecca and Medina.

Time Share: A person's right to use a holiday property for defined or definable period of the year in accordance with a time-share contract.

Time-Share Contract: A contract, or set of contracts, concluded in return for a specified amount of money for a period of not less than three years, under which the right to assign one or more holiday properties, or any other right related thereto, is established for a defined or definable period of the year.

Property: A building or a part thereof, meant for residence, to which the rights subject of the contract relates.

Commission: General Authority for Tourism and Antiquities.

Buyer: A natural or corporate person to whom the right under the time-share contract is assigned or established, for the purpose of using the holiday property to his benefit, through transactions under this Law.

Seller: A natural or corporate person establishing, assigning or undertaking to assign the right to use the holiday property subject of the time-share contract on a commercial basis, through transactions under this Law.

Deferred Payment: A form of credit facility.

Regulations: Implementing Regulations of this Law.

Article 2 Licensing to Engage in Time-Share Activities

1. Time-share activities may not be practiced prior to obtaining a license from the Commission, upon meeting the requirements and furnishing the guarantees specified in the Regulations.
2. Time-share activities may not be advertised or marketed unless said advertisement or marketing includes the following:
   a. The Commission's license number for the advertising party.
   b. The possibility of obtaining the document referred to in paragraph (1) of Article (3) of this Law, and the place where said document can be obtained.

Article 3 Seller's Obligations
The Seller shall undertake:

1. To provide whoever requests information on the time-share property with a document containing complete and accurate information on said property in accordance with the details specified in the Regulations. All information is deemed an integral part of the time-share contract.

2. To provide the Commission with a copy of the document referred to in paragraph (1) of this Article for review and approval, prior to advertising the said property or offering it to the public for sale.
3. To notify the Commission and the buyer of any changes to the information provided in said document, prior to concluding the time-share contract. The contract shall explicitly provide for such changes.
4. To enable the buyer to exercise all rights under the time-share contract, including the right to use said property at the time and within the period specified in the contract.
5. To take the appropriate measures to manage, clean and maintain the real property, to keep it in good condition and fit for use throughout the contract term. Annual management and maintenance costs may be collected from the buyer as stated in the contract.

Article 4 Time-Share Contract and its Terms

1. Provisions of this Law shall apply to time-share contracts concluded in the Kingdom of Saudi Arabia as well as time-share contracts concluded outside the Kingdom of Saudi Arabia if the time-share property is located within the Kingdom.
2. The time-share contract prepared by the seller shall fulfill the following conditions:
   a. It shall be in writing.
   b. It shall contain the details specified in the Regulations.
   c. The contract and the document referred to in paragraph (1) of Article 3 of this Law shall be drafted in Arabic. They may be translated into other languages provided that the Arabic version of the contract prevails.

Article 5 Buyer's Rights and Obligations

1. Without prejudice to any right acquired by the buyer under the laws on the nullity of contracts, the buyer shall have the following options:

   a) To withdraw from a time-share contract without giving any reason within ten days as of the date of concluding the contract by both parties or the date of their signing any binding preliminary document. If the tenth day is an official holiday, the period shall be extended to the first following business day.

   b) To revoke the time-share contract within three months starting from the date of concluding the contract by both parties or the date of their signing any binding preliminary document in case the contract does not include the information specified in paragraph (1) of Article 3 of this Law at the time of signing said contract or document. If such information is provided within the three month period, the buyer's withdrawal period set forth in paragraph (a) of this Article shall commence from the date th information is provided.

   c) To withdraw from the time-share contract without giving any reason within ten days following the lapse of the three months set forth in paragraph (b) of this Article, if the information specified in paragraph (1) of Article 3 of this Law is not provided within the three month period.

2. If the buyer desires to revoke or withdraw from a time-share contract pursuant to paragraph (1) of this Article, he shall, within the specified period, notify the other contracting party or his representative in writing at the address stated in the contract, in the form and by the means stipulated in the Regulations. Said notification shall deemed to be delivered within the specified period if sent prior to the expiry of such period.

3. If the buyer revokes or withdraws from a contract pursuant to paragraph (1) of this Article, he shall not bear any expenses incurred by the seller in relation to the contract.

4. In case of the buyer's death, his right in the time-share contract shall pass to his heirs. The buyer may sell, assign, grant or bequeath his right in the time-share contract and any other rights related thereto.

Article 6 Advance Payments

No advance payment shall be required prior to the end of the period during which the buyer may withdraw from or revoke the contract, pursuant to paragraph (1) of Article 5 of this Law.

Article 7 Revocation of Deferred Payment Agreements

If the price of the time-share contract is fully or partly covered by a deferred payment granted by the seller to the buyer or granted the buyer by a third party–on the basis of a deferred payment agreement between the third party and the seller– and if the buyer withdraws from or revokes the contract pursuant to paragraph (1) of Article 5 of this Law, the deferred payment agreement shall be deemed revoked, without any obligation or liability on the part of the buyer. The Regulations shall set forth the regulatory provisions thereof.

Article 8 No Agreement Contrary to this Law

Any assignment by the buyer to the seller of any of the rights granted under this Law or relieving him from any obligations arising out of this Law shall be deemed null and void.

Article 9 Recording Violations

Officials–to be appointed pursuant to a decision by the Commission's Secretary General–shall monitor the activities of licensees and ensure compliance with conditions and controls. To this end, the officials shall have the right to access records and obtain the information they require. If they discover violations, they shall record such violations and refer them to the committee provided for in paragraph (1) of Article (10) of this Law.

Article 10 Investigating and Deciding Violations

1. Pursuant to a decision by the Chairman's Board of Directors, one or more committees shall be formed of not less than three members, one of whom shall be a legal advisor. The committee shall review violations of the provisions of this Law and impose penalties set forth herein. The committee's decisions shall be approved by the Commission's Secretary General. The Regulations shall state the work procedures of this committee.
2. Appeals from the Committee's decisions may be filed with the Board of Grievances within sixty days from the notification date.

Article 11 Penalties

Without prejudice to any more sever penalty provided for in another law, and without impinging on the rights of others:

1. Any person violating paragraph (1) of Article 2 of this Law shall be subject to a fine not exceeding five hundred thousand riyals.
2. Any person violating paragraph (4) of Article 3 of this Law shall be subject to a fine not exceeding five hundred thousand riyals or revocation of the license, or both penalties.
3. Any person violating paragraph (2) of Article 2, paragraphs (2) and (3) of Article 3 or paragraph (2) of Article 4 of this Law shall be subject to a fine not exceeding three hundred thousand riyals, a maximum one year license suspension or both penalties.
4. Any person violating paragraph (1) of Article 3 of this Law shall be subject to a fine not exceeding one hundred and fifty thousand riyals, a six month license suspension or both penalties.
5. Where no penalty is provided form any person violating any provision of this Law shall be subject to a fine not exceeding one hundred thousand riyals.
6. In case of repetition of any of the violations provided for in this Law, the maximum penalty may be doubled.

Article 12 General Provisions

1. The Commission shall create a record for time-share activities, including detailed information on time-share contracts, sellers, buyers and properties in the Kingdom of Saudi Arabia dedicated to the said activities, in accordance with the Implementing Regulations.
2. Where no provision is made in this Law, the committee set forth in paragraph (1) of Article (10) of this Law shall apply the general rules of contract which regulate the rights and obligations of the contracting parties.
3. Those engaged in time-share activities shall readapt to this Law and amend their termsin accordance with its provisions, within one year from the effective date of this Law.
4. The Commission shall charge for services rendered in accordance with the provisions of this Law, provided that said services and the financial charges are specified by a Council of Ministers Resolution, based on a proposal from the Commission.
5. The Chairman of the Commission's Board of Directors shall issue the Implementing Regulations within ninety days from the date of issuance of this Law.
6. This Law shall be published in the Official Gazette and shall become effective ninety days after its publication.

I.12   The Fallow Lands Distribution Law

Royal Decree No. 26, dated 6/7/1388H (29/9/1968)

Article (1)

The fallow lands in the provisions of Law are intended to mean every land meeting the following terms:

(1) Shall be free of proprietorship jurisdiction rights.

(2) The economical feasibility of its exploitation in agricultural or animal production shall be proven.

(3) Shall be beyond boundaries of physical construction areas and whatsoever pertains to its interests in cities and villages and such shall be specified by the mutual agreement of the Ministries of Interior & Agriculture.

Article 2

The Ministry of Agriculture shall distribute lands to those qualified to exploit such pursuant to the prescribed rules of this Law, provided that the distributed area shall not be less than 5 hectares in each case, and shall not exceed 10 hectares in case of distribution to individuals or 400 hectares. In case of distribution to companies, whereas it shall be permissible to surpass the mentioned limits vide a decision from the Council of Ministers.

Article 3

Whosoever meets the terms hereunder shall be considered qualified to exploit the fallow lands:

(1) Shall be a Saudi National, and such term may be overlooked by a decision from the Council of Ministers.
(2) Shall be enjoying the performance capacity.
(3) Has not, according to this Law, obtained a land with a proven entitlement to its proprietorship.

Article 4

In distributing lands pursuant to this Law, preference shall be effected in the order hereunder:

(1) Proprietor of the land adjacent to the fallow lands subject to distribution.
(2) The Area citizenry.
(3) The most financially capable to invest.

(4) Agriculture professionals.
(5) Whosoever owns no land.

Article 5

Plots of land to be distributed pursuant to this Law shall be specified by the competent authority at the Ministry of Agriculture & Water, and such shall be distributed by a decision from the Minister of Agriculture & Water based on the proposal of a commission comprised of:

(1) Representative of the Ministry of Agriculture & Water.
(2) Representative of the Ministry of Interior.
(3) Representative of the Ministry of Finance & National Economy.
(4) Representative of the Judiciary Presidency designated by the Chief Justice.
(5) Two members renowned of their thorough knowledge and experience of the Area.

The Appointment of the member officials shall be made by a decision from the competent Minister, whereas the appointment of the two members renowned of thorough knowledge and experience shall be made by a decision from the Minister of Agriculture & Water; and it shall be obligatory, prior to issuance of the distribution decision , to affirm that the land subject of distribution shall be devoid of others' right by announcing the intention of distribution in the broadcasting service and one or more widely circulated Saudi newspapers in the Area wherein such land is located a month at least in advance.

Article 6

It shall be obligatory to indicate, in the distribution decision, the fallow land location, area, boundaries (pursuant to a map attached to the decision) and the specified term of its exploitation in agricultural and animal production, and such term shall not be less than two years and not exceed three years.

Article 7

Issuance of the indicated decision shall entail the effects hereunder:

(1) Whosoever has a distribution decision issued in his favor shall have the jurisdiction of the distribution subject land.

(2) It shall be obligatory for the distribution beneficiary to invest on the land within the specified term, and the land shall be considered as agriculturally exploited by irrigating 25% of its area facilitating actual production, and shall be considered as animal stock exploited if such is proven during the specified term of investment.

(3) Whosoever has the distribution decision issued in his favor shall be entitled to the proprietorship of the land pursuant to the rules of this Law.

Article 8

The Ministry of Agriculture shall be entitled to technically supervise the distributed lands, and monitor the seriousness of those with the jurisdiction of investing such, and it shall be permissible, by a decision from the Minister of Agriculture, to cancel jurisdiction of whomsoever proves unable to exploit, or unserious in exploiting , the land during the specified term pursuant to months of serving him notice, and such shall be allocated to two another person after paying his predecessor his actual expenses, provided that when redistributing the land, the new investor shall be committed to compensate his predecessor the increased value of the land due to the efforts exerted therein.

Article 9

If whosoever the distribution decision was issued in his favor exploits the land, and the specified term of investment elapses, enforcement of such shall be his entitlement by a decision from the

Minister of Agriculture, but such decision shall not be effective unless approved by his Majesty the King or whosoever he delegates.

Article 10

A Committee of representatives of the Ministry of Agriculture, Ministry of Justice, Ministry of Interior and the Ministry of water, are of such representatives shall be a legal counsel, shall be formed at the Ministry of Agriculture to examine any disputes arising from the execution of the provisions of this Law, the decisions of such Committee shall be sanctioned by the Minister of Agriculture, and whoever being affected by a decision of such Committee may complain before the Board of Grievances within sixty days of his notification of such.

Article 11

The provisions stipulated in Article (9) shall be applicable to the waste lands apportioned by the ruler prior to the issuance of this Law, and their beneficiaries' entitlement to their proprietorship has not been proven.

Article 12

The Minister of Agriculture & Water shall issue the implementing regulations of this Law.

INDEX

ABOUT THE AUTHOR

Michael O'Kane is an attorney with twelve years experience in Saudi Arabia and the Middle East. He is a former special legal advisor to the Kingdom of Saudi Arabia and in that capacity drafted a legal code, including a disputes resolution code, for the Kingdom's Economic Cities project. More recently he has been advising the Saudi Railways Commission on licensing and regulating the growing rail sector in the Kingdom and has assisted them in drafting regulations for an administrative tribunal to resolve disputes. He is currently senior counsel with Charles Russell LLP as part of the firm's Saudi project. Previously he was with Blake, Cassels & Graydon, LLP based in Al Khobar and before that Freshfields Bruckhaus Deringer in Riyadh. His book, Doing Business in Saudi Arabia is #20 on Amazon's International Law bestseller list. He has also written two other books on Saudi law, Saudi Labor Law Outline and more recently, Saudi Securities Law. He also edited a handbook on Iraqi law.

In the United States federal courts he tried in excess of twenty five cases to verdict and has handled both domestic as well as international litigation. Today his practice involves corporate and commercial matters, due diligence, managing foreign and domestic investigations and anti-corruption compliance.

He is admitted to practice in three different U.S. state jurisdictions. Following his successful defense of a codefendant in United States v. Noriega, he has been practicing law in the Middle East.

www.ingramcontent.com/pod-product-compliance
Lightning Source LLC
Chambersburg PA
CBHW060349220326
41598CB00023B/2850